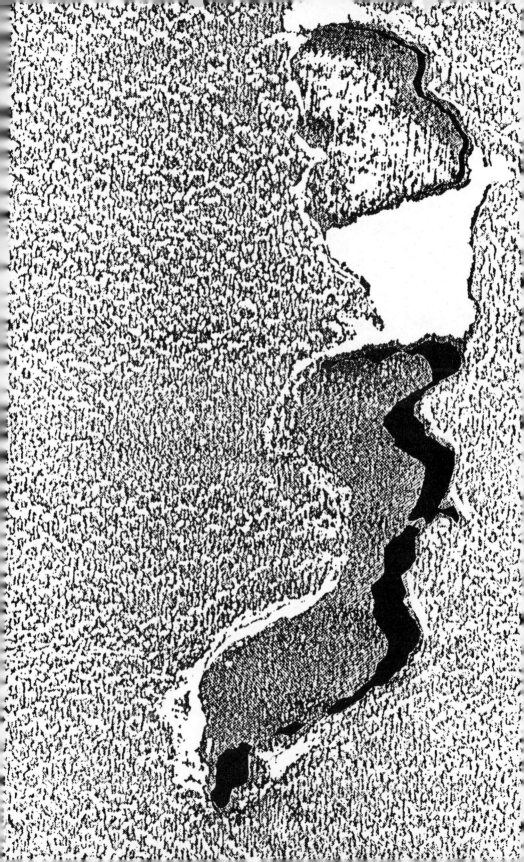

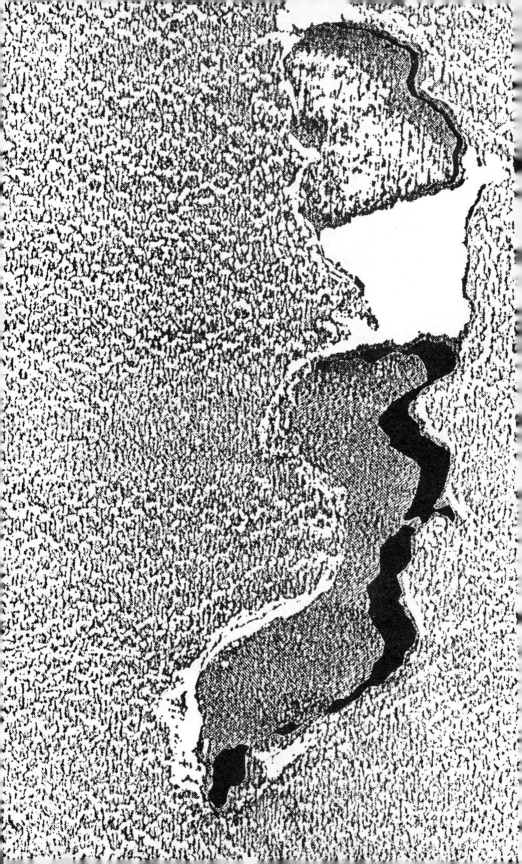

IN NICARAGUA

So many conflicting things are written about Nicaragua that it is hard to know whom to trust. Joel Kovel has made several trips there and has worked among the people, particularly in the sensitive area of mental illness. This book is a sustained reflection on his experiences – thoughtful, honest, perceptive.

He brings to the subject his experience as a careful observer of the social history of people in distress. His previous books include *A Complete Guide to Therapy*; *The Age of Desire*; and, published by Free Association Books, *The Radical Spirit: Essays on Psychoanalysis and Society*; *White Racism: A Psychohistory*; and *Against the State of Nuclear Terror*.

One of his main preoccupations is the critique of oppressive bureaucracies and the ways they limit human freedom. The chapter on his dealings with an American Embassy official is a revealing and funny story of how power and position can so transform a person's perceptions that they cannot see what is before their eyes. In another essay, he walks about among the people and provides a vivid account of the atmosphere – the strengths and weaknesses – of Sandinista Nicaragua.

Joel Kovel is a psychoanalyst who has written widely on social, cultural and political aspects of human nature, always treating them as inside history. He has held posts in psychiatry, social theory and history at Yeshiva University, New York, the New School for Social Research, New York, and the University of California. He has held a Guggenheim Fellowship and the Alger Hiss Professorship of Social Studies at Bard College, New York State.

IN NICARAGUA

JOEL KOVEL

'an association in which the free development of each
is the condition of the free development of all'

Free Association Books / London / 1988

First published in Great Britain in 1988 by
Free Association Books
26 Freegrove Road
London N7 9RQ

British Library Cataloguing in Publication Data

Kovel, Joel
  In Nicaragua.
  1. Nicaragua. Revolutionary movements
  I. Title
  322.4'2'097285
  ISBN 0 946960 90 9
  ISBN 0 946960 91 7 pbk

Typeset by Columns of Reading

Printed and bound in Great Britain by
Bookcraft, Midsomer Norton, Avon

To Solmaría, Joaquín Antonio and baby Bayardo Arce

CONTENTS

ACKNOWLEDGEMENTS

A work such as this is particularly dependent on others, and I cannot hope to thank adequately all the people who have given it support, both in Nicaragua and the United States. Within Nicaragua, my stay was made possible by the kindness and generosity of many people. I am especially grateful to Ezra Halleck, Kenia Vega Sacasa, the family of Julia Cuadra de Sacasa, and Pedro Joaquín and Ligia Romero. Also, Peter Halleck, Dr Mario Flores Ortíz, Elsa Ruth Ugarte, Rita Arauz, Peter Marchetti, Judy Butler, Freddy Balzan, Edwige Balutansky, María de Zúñiga, Indiana Acevedo, Soledad McIntyre, Dr Ligia Altamirano, Howard Hiner, Paul Jeffries, Jim and Margaret Goff, Vilma Castillo, June Mulligan, Jorge Margolis, Xavier Vicenzio, the Cooperatives of Gamez–Garmendia, Yvonne Rodríguez, José González, Hazel Lau and César Pais. For the development of this manuscript I am indebted to Adam Friedson for his active support, and to Robert Young for his encouragement and forbearance. I am also grateful to Steve Cagan, Martin Lucas, Martha Wallner, Elsa First, Grace Paley and Bob Nichols, Russell Jacoby, and Sandra Dijkstra. And once more and throughout, to my main critic and support, Dee Dee Halleck.

PREFACE

In Nicaragua is a memoir, first composed as a journal during a visit in 1986, then reworked during the months following my return. Now, a year or so later, the Nicaragua described in the text has already moved on, just as the Nicaragua mused about in this preface will be different from how Nicaragua will be when this book is read. History in Nicaragua lurches onwards, and the only certainty is turmoil. One does not experience Nicaragua like Venice, or the British countryside, or other places defined by tradition. There is a past, a shameful past to most Nicaraguans, but it lies in shreds, or cruelly tries to destroy the new nation from without. Inside, in the Nicaragua I tried to know, the past is no longer a framework. Revolutions are obliged to either overcome or annihilate tradition. In either case, little remains to check the free fall into the future.

And Nicaragua freely falls. Freely, for there is no place on earth more uncertain of outcome. And falls, under the brutal pressures of underdevelopment and the counter-revolutionary war launched by the violent superpower which happens to be my homeland. Since I first became directly acquainted with the country, late in 1983, two sayings have been consistently true about Nicaragua: first, 'the economic situation is deteriorating', and second, that the 'next few weeks/months are critical'. It can be no surprise, then, that the hardships described here have got worse. Some instances: when I was last there, in 1986, the córdoba fetched 2,000 to the dollar on the black market – an appalling increase over previous visits. A month ago, I heard it was going for 30,000. I am afraid to ask the rate now. Again, in 1986 I had to put up with bad water-shortages, a reasonably erratic power supply, and petrol whose availability was subject merely to the nuisance of getting coupons. Today, the water supply is worse (three days a week without water instead of two), the power is shut down for six hours each day, and huge queues adorn the petrol stations. I also learn that the Diplo store, which is the first setting described in the narrative, is now one of a chain of stores frantically resorted to by the government in order to squeeze some dollars from, as well as provide some material succour to, the international community. In sum, the economy is collapsing. There is little telling how far this collapse can or need go, for an economy is not something which goes out like a light. But there is no question that the situation has gone from terrible to desperate.

In the mean while, the people have held on, as more contra aid was passed, the Arias Peace Plan materialized, the Nicaraguan government made a rash of concessions, and the anti-intervention movement in the United States kept up its drumbeat. As I write, that pusillanimous body, the House of Representatives, has actually denied to the President his latest contra aid package. A significant moment, beyond doubt, but scarcely the last crisis, or the end of Nicaragua's time on the cross. Many opportunities still lie open to the malevolence of the *ancien régime*.

How it will turn out for Nicaragua is not to be predicted here. Despite everything, I remain hopeful, which is neither here nor there except as a reminder that this is a book written by someone who tends to be hopeful about such things. Let us say, critically hopeful; Gramsci's call for pessimism of the intellect and optimism of the will strikes the right chord for me. The tension between these poles may be said to define the spirit of *In Nicaragua*; that, and a bearing of witness to the inchoate day-by-day life of a revolution, beneath the level of ideologies and the grand sweep of historical forces. From the standpoint of Nicaragua as a nation, the Sandinista revolution marks the birth of an authentic and irrevocable national identity. From the standpoint of world history, it reveals an elemental shift of power away from the traditional centre of US imperialism. But from an everyday standpoint, as individuals contend with immediate existence, these great forces are often obscure. None the less they play themselves out in every detail. We always live history; but those who engage in a revolution live it more insistently, even if at times more confusedly and darkly. Virtues and flaws alike are drawn more sharply and exaggerated under revolutionary conditions. For there is no reason why a revolution should appear sensible and consistently virtuous on the ground. Indeed, there is every reason to expect it to be full of nonsense as well as violations of accepted canons.

And yet I think the mess of life lived in a revolution may be truer to reality than the order of bourgeois democracy. At least it is if we take seriously the notion that conflict is the mother of all things. A revolution epitomizes the Heraclitean stream into which one can never step twice. It is closer, then, to the stuff of the world than the illusions of stability we ordinarily crave. This is why, I think, so many feel more alive in the bad air of Managua or under the enormous travail of life in the countryside, struggling with the seemingly impossible job of building a new society in the teeth of Uncle Sam's hatred.

In Nicaragua is by the same token also a narrative of estrangement. I do not represent the Nicaraguan people whose cause I adopt, and I belong deeply to a society with whose basic policies I feel deeply at odds. In this sense the views expressed in this book differ from those of the majority of my fellow citizens who have opposed the US government's policies towards Central America. It is perfectly understandable, on moral, political and legal grounds, to oppose the murderousness of the US security apparatus in Nicaragua without at the same time supporting the Sandinista revolution. There is no necessary connection between the two positions. Indeed, Americans who oppose Reagan in Central America often feel a certain distaste for the Sandinistas. No doubt this is nourished by the flood of odium poured forth by our subservient press; but this fact does not imply any necessity to support the Sandinistas either. After all, it is perfectly clear that not all the miseries of Nicaragua can be blamed on Ronald Reagan and Elliott Abrams, Undersecretary of State in charge of destroying the revolution.

And yet I do support the Sandinistas. Or, as I try to make clear in the text, I support the revolution, and the Sandinistas as those who have taken responsibility for the revolution. There are many reasons for this, but it is, finally, an existential stand, like love or religious belief. As such, it cannot be logically justified, but only indicated. I do not deny the existence of logical justifications for supporting a revolution. In fact, I imagine myself capable of spelling them out. But I also think that the effective reason why a person goes one way politically or another – the efficient cause of the belief, if you will – is non-rational; not necessarily irrational, but non-rational. It belongs to the cloudy realm of will and faith, where history and an individual existence intersect. I try to draw back the clouds a bit in the text, though it is doubtful whether I succeed in fully doing so. Can we ever truly express our immediately lived reality in writing? I think not . . . which is one reason to keep on writing. In any case, I will be always grateful to Nicaragua for allowing me to share some of my life with it, and to express in this halting way some of the love I feel for the land and its people.

February 1988

THE
MARCH

THE DIPLO STORE is an odious institution, and an embarrass-
ment to the Sandinista revolution. As with so many places in
Managua, it doesn't seem to be anywhere. One turns off the
main road linking the Tiscapa volcano with the Carretera Masaya,
goes up an improbably steep embankment – if one's ancient and
improvised car permits – and through what appears to be a vacant
lot leading nowhere. But then the road turns sharply left, down
another embankment, and suddenly a sleek and neatly kept middle-
class street materializes. There, on the right side, are the newly
minted parking spaces installed to accommodate the rush of people
with credentials and, critically, dollars who come seeking commodities. The street in front of the Diplo store may be the only
place in Nicaragua where parking is scarce. Where else can one get
Nestlé's Crunch, Kellogg's Sugar Frosted Flakes, or a General
Electric Freezer? All this and much, much more is trucked in from
Panama by an enterprise half-private and half-governmental, that
does well by doing good for the affluent international community,
the corps of journalists who watch the country like vultures and,
perhaps most importantly, for Nicaragua's unhappy rich, who
depart daily for Miami, leaving this land forsaken by the reigning
economic system. The government reasons that they will not leave
as precipitously, taking their skills and capital with them, if there is
a store where they can buy good Scott's toilet paper, at one dollar

the roll, instead of the green and inconstant issue which is the Nicaraguan's standard lot.

It is the same logic which leads the authorities to stock their television channels with markedly unrevolutionary Mexican and Brazilian soap operas, the former depicting *fin-de-siècle* upper-class romantic intrigue, the latter, the same subjects in the era of Porsches, bikinis, and heated swimming pools. These programmes are clearly the favourites of that tenth or so of the population which has access to television. One of these is a teacher at the American School here, who recently bought, for 13,000 dollars, a deserted hacienda on sixty acres of the gradually ascending and gorgeous land south of the city. Here he lives like a lord, amid views extending across Lake Managua and the mountains beyond for one hundred miles, surrounded by people many of whom have never known shoes in the fifty years of life allotted to them by poverty. But he is a kindly man who has been touched by the spirit of the revolution; and so he gives his tenants excellent terms, opens his house to them in the evening, and serves them popcorn while they ritually watch the soap operas.

I had gone to the Diplo store to buy a gift for Joaquín Antonio, and for Pedro Joaquín and Ligia, his parents and my hosts for the last four of my nine-week stay in Nicaragua. These were the official reasons which got me over my aversion to the Diplo store, but there were others – to be specific, curiosity to experience my culture again, and a craving for chocolate. I had not tasted chocolate for a month, save for one small chocolate bar, from a stash delivered by a visiting Northamerican to my stepson, Ezra. Once I saw a chocolate bar of oriental design in a supermarket. I learned later that the People's Republic of China, with whom Nicaragua had just established diplomatic relations, had blessed its new friend with a shipment of chocolate, along with other delights, such as freeze-dried Chinese delicacies. But I had let the chance to purchase slip by, because of the long queue, and when I returned, the goods were gone, the ship had long since left, and the new one was yet to arrive. Now, however, surrounded by, wallowing in, commodities, I could choose from between more than twenty varieties, from bags of Hershey's Kisses to elegant flat packages of Swiss chocolates, each with a picture of a different Alp on the outside. Just like home. The sight numbed me, then terrified me. I wanted to run, but stayed, remembering Joaquín Antonio.

The toy department was worse than the food department. There seemed to be nothing but robots with machine-guns and, for the little ladies, cherubic pink dolls with yellow hair. Finally I found a model of a back-hoe, made in Spain, for the boy, and emboldened by my success, some French pâté and English jam to replace the luxury goods I had consumed from Pedro and Ligia's scarce larder. I turned next to the drinks department, where there are some excellent buys. I was about to purchase a bottle of Drambuie when I recalled a conversation with Pedro Joaquín in which he evinced an uncommon interest in Alcoholics Anonymous. Prudence stayed my hand and gave me the wit to choose instead a small bar of Cadbury's Milk Chocolate for my personal treat.

But the Managua sun was unkind to the chocolate, or perhaps it was my long abstinence. The candy failed to satisfy. It only brought into sharper relief what I had been longing for: not delicacies, but food itself. Forty-eight hours before my departure from the land of Sandino, I realized that, like the rest of the Nicaraguan people with whom I had been sharing this fragment of life, I was chronically hungry. I had plenty of money, indeed, was quite wealthy by Nicaraguan standards. Yet what good was money when there was simply not enough food to buy, when the restaurants had less and less to serve and the portions seemingly withered away on the plate before one's eyes? There had been occasions when hunger had led me to order two meals for myself. My body clamoured for protein, not a confection. As if in response, I pulled on my belt. Sure enough, it went in another notch.

What was I doing in Nicaragua? Ostensibly, working with the Ministerio de Salud Mental as an *internacionalista*, a volunteer expert from abroad. I had been to Nicaragua for brief visits in 1983, 1984 and 1985, and had felt that sharp tug common to many of the more than 100,000 Northamericans (we may call ourselves Americans, but to the other inhabitants of the hemisphere, this is another example of chauvinism; they call us Northamericans, unfortunately roping Canada in with the United States, and I shall respect that usage here) who troop through and gaze at the revolution so hated by the regime of Ronald Reagan. Like many others, I had wanted to do more than gaze. When a sabbatical leave from my Department of Psychiatry gave me the opportunity, I seized it.

I went to Nicaragua to help, because this is the only legitimate reason for eating their scarce food and burning their scarce fuel. But I went also in the spirit of curiosity. I wanted to learn a little more of what life was like on the ground there. I found after my first trips that I could spout a lot of the facts of the revolution, but that the lived reality of it quite eluded me. There had been glimpses, but they disappeared like a deer into the forest. I went with no thought of forming a comprehensive view of the society – who ever gets a comprehensive view of a society? It was simply a desire to be present and explore something of the raw and immediate life of Nicaragua. Perhaps, too, I was feeling frustrated by having to repeat the usual catechism of debating points about the revolution: so many benefits here, so many flaws there. Are the Sandinistas persecuting the Miskitu Indians, or have they mended their ways? Do they have direct democracy, or have they 'abandoned the goals of the revolution'? Do the gains in health care (usually measured as changes in infant mortality or the rate of various diseases, or the number of new clinics) or education (usually measured as rates of literacy) outweigh the losses in freedom of the press or political pluralism? And are these losses to be accounted for as responses to US aggression, Soviet penetration, or the inevitable concomitants of a one-party state? Are the Sandinistas 'Marxist-Leninists', or Christian revolutionaries, or pragmatic opportunists or . . . ?

I had chewed these questions over countless times, had argued them, read about them, pondered them, and held them to be valid things to know about revolutionary Nicaragua. But they were the kind of things which led one to put up conceptual fences. They were arguments leading toward abstractions; they brought one to a terrain where abstract words – democracy, Marxism, freedom, pluralism, classes – are in the saddle and ride the raw stuff of historical experience. And they tell us nothing of what life is like in Nicaragua.

Mental arrogance makes us prisoners of our own concepts. Caught by our desire to prove ourselves right, we lose sight of the reality we want to be right about, and live in a world of phrases. Nicaragua, where as of this time of writing the United States has all but formally declared war, is a particularly tragic instance of how ideologically loaded words can blind us to reality. This is as true for those of the Left as of the Right, for those who defend the revolution or those who attack it.

Indifference, the notion that Nicaragua is none of one's personal business, is no answer to this problem, although it is the way chosen by the majority of US citizens. We Northamericans may be a politically apathetic people, but we live in, pay taxes to, and reproduce the most dynamic society on earth, the one which makes the greatest difference in the lives of the five billion human passengers on this tiny speck of space-time. Our apathy as a people is a vital part of the way the United States works. And like it or not, the fate of Nicaragua and that of the United States are inextricably bound together. Nicaragua is the business of every Northamerican. One does as much toward Nicaragua by having no interest in it as does the passionate defender or the implacable enemy of Sandinism. And what we do to Nicaragua we also do to ourselves.

So there is a need to find out more about the reality of Nicaragua as it is lived from the inside rather than observed from the outside. Nicaragua may be the most scrutinized nation in history – certainly as a function of size – but it is almost always looked at as though it were a patient with some mysterious disease who submits itself to the gaze of a legion of medical experts. I wanted to find out what the lived world of Nicaragua was like, not as disease but as revolution. And so I went, driven by that obscure tug, to live in Nicaragua a while, to work, share in the life and observe what happened. Of course I would be a partisan observer, and a partial one. I could only see things through my eyes and my own conceptual filters. But if we waited for a pure or full observation, we would never know anything about human society.

Except for my volunteer status in the mental health system and a press card I eventually wangled through the auspices of an influential friend, I had no official standing in Nicaragua. And so I came to the end of my nine-week stay without meeting or interviewing a Comandante of the revolution. I did, however, come close once to being trampled by Daniel Ortega.

The Roberto Huembes market sits like a gigantic turtle on the edge of the shapeless eastern barrios of Managua. Under its spreading brown roof work hundreds of small merchants, tortilla-makers and repair shops. In front of the market is a major depot from which perilously overcrowded and decrepit buses depart for points south; in the back is one of the innumerable vacant lots of the city. One day, perhaps, many of these will be parks. Now, in the time of hardship, the lots become like the spaces between the pieces of an unmade jigsaw puzzle scattered about the gently rising land to the south of Lake Managua. On the evening of 27 June 1986, in a dusk made darker by the remnants of a light rain, about 60,000 people were gathered in this space. They were there to listen to the leadership of the revolution and to participate in the seventh annual re-enactment of the *repliegue*, a word which literally means 'a folding' or 'doubling up' but may be best translated in its Nicaraguan context as 'tactical retreat'.

On the same evening in 1979, the people of the eastern barrios found themselves encircled by the forces of the soon-to-be-deposed dictator, Anastasio Somoza. The insurrection that had taken seventeen years was in its agonizing last stage. The final outcome was by now certain, but Somoza, like a wounded and crazed beast, was doing all he could to annihilate the rising masses who were about to overthrow him. The eastern barrios had been a focus of militancy, just as they had been a zone of almost unrelieved poverty and squalor, and the dictator was going to stop at nothing to turn his tanks and planes against the people who lived there. Most of the 50,000 deaths of the insurrection took place in the closing months of almost continual uprising, and the number would have been significantly greater had Somoza caught the eastern barrios in his noose. But an escape route was discovered, and during the night of 27 June, about six thousand people slipped away, and walked some thirty kilometres over the back roads to Masaya, the next town of any size to the south. There they regrouped and returned to the capital for the final struggle. The two great mythological themes of Nicaraguan life are martyrdom and redemption. The exodus of 27 June 1979 is for the Nicaraguans their reliving of the Exodus of the children of Israel out of Egypt and toward freedom; it was a sign of their redemption as a people, and they commemorate it fervidly each year.

On this 27 June about 50,000 of the 60,000 celebrants seemed to me to be youths below the age of twenty. Many were dressed in plain olive-green militia uniform. They formed human chains that snaked through the crowd and human pyramids that rose above it as they waited for the *repliegue* to begin. I was there, too, having come with Pedro Joaquín from his home in barrio 14 Septiembre, with a poncho folded in my trouser pocket, a canteen of Managua tap water tied by coarse twine to my belt, and in my shirt pocket a plastic bag of tortillas supplied by Liliana, the *campesina* (peasant woman) from Estelí who cared for Pedro Joaquín's home and her five-month-old baby, Bayardo Arce. 14 Septiembre had been one of the militant eastern barrios, and Pedro had been second-in-command of the insurrection there. He had been on the original *repliegue* and on several since. This year, because of several all-night meetings in the days around 27 June, he had not planned to go, but the United States House of Representatives changed his mind for him when it collapsed before Reagan's tirade against Nicaragua and approved 110 million dollars in aid to the counter-revolution. Pedro went, therefore, in rage, as did many another Nicaraguan. The crowd was larger and more militant than ever as it gathered before the makeshift podium, on which were already uncomfortably arrayed members of the international diplomatic corps, and awaited the arrival of President Daniel Ortega, who was to address and lead the march.

It may be, as Hegel and others have said, that history is made by spirit; but spirit acts through flesh which is, in the words of Blake, its chief inlet in the modern age. And the flesh which embodied my spirit was declining as fast as the light when Ortega, scowling as usual, pulled up in his jeep with Vice-President Sergio Ramírez, Comandantes Carlos Núñez and Luis Carrión and their retinue, to begin the ceremonies.

It is hard to stay well for long in sultry Managua, especially when the rainy season, which begins in mid-May, brings a pestilential invasion of flies, while the water supply, stretched thin by the fulminant growth of the city, has to be shut off two days a week. I had done reasonably well for the first month of my stay, when I lived alone, but now, living in the household of Pedro Joaquín and sharing its life, I had become radically more exposed. I am sorry, too, to say that the Nicaraguan cuisine is not the world's most salubrious, being composed of a high percentage of grease; while as for Liliana, though a rock-like woman who commanded my respect for her sincerity, industry, good faith and good cheer, candour compels me to report that the culinary arts were not among her repertoire of skills. Several weeks of eating unidentifiable and unchewable substances, served with dry white bread and over-sweet black coffee, had sapped my resistance. To this background had to be added some days of severe defeats at the hands of the amazing Nicaraguan bureaucracy, which seemed bent on thwarting my plans and for good measure driving me mad.

Beyond all this, I think I had been made ill by my reaction to the news of the vote. Nicaraguans tend to be insouciant by national character, and have, in any case, no burden of responsibility for the behaviour of the US government. For Northamericans living in Nicaragua, a cleansing rage at Ronald Reagan is impossible to achieve. One cannot escape some degree of identity with one's country by blaming it all on the men in command. Not guilt, but some residue of shame, lingers. When the news of the vote reached us, I was at a party. The Nicaraguans heard it, shrugged, and went back to dancing and laughing, while I slumped into a chair and fell into a morbid reverie. '¿Qué pasa, hermano?' I was asked solicitously by people who could not imagine taking the acts of barbarians to heart. 'What's the matter, brother?'

As Ortega stepped to the microphone, I still wasn't sure what was the matter. I only knew that something was very wrong with the middle section of my body. It began to occur to me that the issue had become less being able to endure the *repliegue*, an experience 'muy duro, pero muy lindo' (hard but beautiful) as a Nicaraguan friend had told me, than of gathering enough strength to get back to Pedro Joaquín's house, where I could collapse in peace on my narrow army cot. The waves of pain radiating from my solar plexus were driving gangrenous vapour upward from my stomach and making my legs give out from beneath me. It seemed I would not have the strength to go that far. I thought next of staggering to Peter Rosset's house, which was the closest place I knew, to rest enough to get back to barrio 14 Septiembre. But what if he wasn't there? This rumination was mooted by a fresh surge of

8

pain and weakness. Now I could only think of staggering to the edge of the crowd, where I might find enough unoccupied turf to rest upon. Sadly, I gave my tortillas to a companion and wished him well on the *repliegue*. Barely able to stay erect, I wove a path to the outskirts of the throng, cast my poncho on the ground, and lying down, fell into a stupor, my eyes fixed glassily upon the darkening heavens.

I must have been so for half-an-hour, dozing and musing bitterly on the futility of life in Nicaragua, while Ortega addressed the crowd on the consequences of the vote in Congress, the latest wave of contra atrocities and the situation with the suspended pro-Reagan newspaper, *La Prensa*. Then a muffled roar broke into my cocoon. I raised my head, focused my gaze . . . and beheld a mass of humanity moving like a tidal wave in my direction. The *repliegue* had begun and I was lying in its path. More particularly, I was lying in the path of Daniel Ortega, who was heading toward my inert form at an excellent pace, followed by Ramírez, Núñez and Carrión, their bodyguards, the press and video crews, several jeeps and 60,000 chanting Nicaraguans. I doubt that Ortega would have actually trampled me if he had seen me. On the other hand, I doubt that he would have seen me in time to stop, given the man's velocity and determination. In either case, I had no thought of putting the matter to a test. In fact, I had no thought at all. The reflexes of survival took command of the situation, lurching me on rubbery legs to my feet, poncho in hand.

I then began to think, and the first thought was that I was by no means out of danger. Ortega and the leadership had passed, but the crowd behind them was like a solid wall, made denser by its passage out of the field and onto the road. Everyone seemed to be pushing everyone else in their eagerness to stay with the leaders, and all were obviously in a rapt frame of mind which had no room for consideration of an unwell gringo in their path. My sluggish body was picked up by this mass as if it were a chip of wood in a flashflood. Recollections of people crushed by mobs flashed across my rapidly clearing sensibility, as it occurred to me that I might very well end my life on the edge of that field behind the Huembes market.

There was an irony in this which I was in no mood to appreciate at the time. No one can travel in Nicaragua today without awareness of the possibility that life-threatening violence can break out at any time. The streets of Managua are proverbially safe (though there has been a disturbing emergence lately of youth gangs), and one never feels the least bit threatened by the Sandinista police, those intensely serious and unarmed young men, all seemingly eighteen-years-old, five feet, ten inches tall, weighing 130 pounds, and exuding revolutionary morality. Nor is there any sense of fear lest some of the innumerable armed patrols – again, many of them extraordinarily young – should become trigger happy, or regard a gringo as a *yanqui* and vent their anger on him. But this is a war waged by terrorist bands whose prime targets are civilians; and it is a war which could bring a US bombing raid *à la* Libya, or even a full-scale invasion, at any time. Standard table-talk in Nicaragua includes speculation on what to do in the event of the invasion, which is increasingly viewed as inevitable. (Stay away from the US Embassy – on moral grounds, and because it surely will be plastered by the Sandinistas – and find some other neutral ground, for me, the Peruvian Embassy, where I had friends.)

It had also occurred to me that a death in Nicaragua at the hands of Ronald Reagan's armies would not be a death without value for a citizen of the United States of America, whence it is axiomatic that a contra would never kill, deliberately at any rate, a Northamerican.* A death by trampling under a mass of Sandinista youth, on the other hand – what a catastrophe that would be for the friends of Nicaragua!

In any event, I was not about to let this happen. Now the only way to survive a fast-moving crowd like this is to move with it, passively at first, like the chip on the flood, and then in synchronization, finding one's rhythm in pace with the marchers. This I did; and so it was that, despite myself, I set forth on the seventh *repliegue* from Managua to Masaya, through the back barrios of the city and the unmarked roads of the countryside, in the cool darkness of a Nicaraguan night.

---

* This was written before the murder of Benjamin Linder, an engineer who lived and worked among the peasants in the north of Nicaragua, by the contras in April 1987.

My stomach still ached, but differently. The pain was no longer *me* but in me, and it had been locked up for the moment. Indeed, the further I went, the easier it seemed. I was encouraged too by the fact that the march would pass very close by Pedro Joaquín's house within the first kilometre, which meant that an escape route was at hand. By now the crowd had become diluted to the point of being able to see spaces between individuals (though everybody was continually bumping into and tripping over everybody else). I could begin to observe my surroundings and the marchers. We were on the straight, wide and unnamed street (scarcely any street in Managua is named) which led from the Huembes market to the turn-off to Pedro's house. I knew it as the street with the missing manhole-cover. Though this scarcely qualified as a unique description of a Managua thoroughfare, it had the practical value of reminding me that my car – and now my person – could at any moment disappear into an abyss. Eternal vigilance is the price of Managua travel. In this case the trap was the more insidious in that the cover had been replaced for a few days, then mysteriously removed again. I would not really begin to concentrate on my fellow marchers until this menace was safely behind me. The air was smoky from numerous bonfires and the figures were indistinct, but I began to make them out. And there, next to me striding rapidly in the haze, was a form I knew: stocky, bearded, bespectacled, with a baseball cap, canteen and what looked like a Boy Scout rucksack bouncing up and down on his back, his chin set, leaning forward, marching determinedly . . .

'¡Pedro, compañero! ¡Hola!'

'¿Qué tal? Caminaremos juntos.' We will walk together.

Now there would be no turning back from the *repliegue*. I was going to make it or collapse trying, and from that moment, forgot about my health. At the end of the street with the missing manhole-cover, one turns left to get to Pedro's house. We turned right, with the march, and as we did, I saw a youth, bare-chested, disappear into one of the city's innumerable grateless sewers (so common one would never think of identifying a street by the fact, only of staying away from the sides). He rose, Lazarus-like, and rejoined the march.

The scene could only have been captured by a Goya. The eastern

11

barrios, so drab and poor by day, were now bathed in orange, red and white light, pungent from burning tyres and palm fronds, and festooned with banners urging the marchers on and condemning the 100 million dollars. They needed no urging. They held no formation, but bumped, stumbled, ran, joined hands, went on each other's shoulders, as an endless solid wall of people stood by the side of the road, watching and cheering. Every so often, a beep would announce a vehicle trying to get through. Usually these were the ubiquitous Toyota Land Cruiser, staple of automotive transportation in the Third World. Once, however, a higher-pitched, tinnier and more insistent beep drew my attention. Turning, I faced a colossal dark green tank, stately as an elephant in a parade and swarming with youngsters, some clinging like ticks, the others hopping on and off. What would the Soviet or East German designers of this leviathan think if they saw it now, clanking through the streets of Managua decked with its cargo of celebrants?

The road abruptly lost its pavement, the lights and onlookers thinned, and we were in the countryside. There is poverty throughout the Nicaraguan *campo*, but integrity and community as well. Managua is nobody's favourite place; indeed, I cannot recall ever hearing a kind word said about this a-centric, earthquake-blighted and generally absurd city. But the countryside is beloved, rolling and incredibly fertile; and it was a pleasure to emerge after an hour of marching through the hectic, acrid city onto the tableland between Managua and Masaya.

The marchers seemed to sober up immediately. They ceased their carousing and settled into a steady rhythm punctuated by an occasional cheer or song. Many – too many for me – of the young people smoked, and the glow of their butts scattered over the road provided a counterpoint of tiny lights to the tramp of boots. Every so often we would pass a dwelling, lit by fire or electricity and converted into an oasis for the sweat-soaked and ever-wearying marchers. Occasionally a light shining upward would illuminate a great spreading Ceiba or Tayacan tree. The effect was celestial, as if the stars had come down to earth and hovered just above us. Now an ambulance approached, its siren wailing. Inside, a thin young man was lying supine and shirtless, an attendant hovering above him. The ambulance passed, and soon its siren ceased. Had it broken down? Was the young man better? Or had he died? Music from an oasis overtook us. It was the Platters, singing 'The Great Pretender', an old favourite of Pedro Joaquín's.

The *repliegue* had become a dreamscape spread over several kilometres of gently undulating back road. But whose dream? It seemed as if each of us, as individuals, no longer marched as or for ourselves. Pedro and I knew we were next to each other, and when, as would often happen, we became momentarily separated by a hurrying or dallying marcher, or because one or the other stumbled on a stone or tripped crossing a rut, we searched for the other's silhouette and hastened to rejoin him. But otherwise there was no way of becoming located in the march.

Figures came and went, perhaps male, perhaps female, mostly young. They were not individuals but our reflections or substitutes. None of us knew where we were, beyond being on the middle or outside of the road, and none knew which way to go, except the way of the marchers in front. If at first I went on because I could always stop at Pedro's house, or turn back to it, now I went on because there was no way back; to stop would mean a night spent lost and unprotected in the countryside. So it seemed as if we were not marching. Rather was the march marching us. I was part of a pair with Pedro Joaquín, but as pair, we, and the thousands of small clusters of individuals, were figures conjured by the nocturnal and collective dream of the Nicaraguan revolution.

After four hours, the leg pain began, and each step became a deliberate act, aggravated by the continual tripping over unseen objects. We didn't want to rest now for fear of stiffening muscles; yet rest we did, by a pair of water trucks providently supplied by the authorities. The tank passed us once more, now completely encrusted with freeloaders, and with legs of wood, we resumed gratefully along a long, descending stretch of straight, smooth road, until we came upon the little town of Nindirí, where an elaborate rest facility had been announced. It was one o'clock in the morning, and we had been marching for five-and-a-half hours.

The rest facility turned out to be a quaint and largely unserviceable park, complete with playground, basketball court and bandstand. There is a peculiar kind of cacophonous music native to this part of Nicaragua which sounds like a cross between Charles Ives,

Kurt Weill and a sack of glass bottles falling downstairs. Somewhere on the podium, hidden behind a mass of swaying marchers, a band was gamely playing some of this music. Recordings of more conventional and sentimental fare followed, the more indefatigable youth dancing and supporting one another as in a marathon dance contest.

Pedro sat down on the steps of a children's playground while I went off to see whether other friends had arrived. When I returned, empty-handed, Pedro was gone. Weary, I laid my poncho down once more, now in a sandbox, and with my canteen as a pillow and surrounded by Sandinistas in various degrees of repose, I slept.

I was awakened by a light rain. With complaining feet, I marched the eight kilometres to Masaya, the final destination of the *repliegue*. Night was fading now, and the road, increasingly settled, was lined once again with folk greeting the march. Masaya is a cheerful town, with rows of pastel-coloured houses taller again by half than the typical Nicaraguan dwelling. Its soft yellows, blues and greens, washed by the morning rain, were punctuated by hundreds of red and black FSLN (Frente Sandinista de Liberación Nacional) banners adorning the walls and fluttering over the marchers. In the plaza, Ortega and the other leaders, fatigued and happy, greet us. 'In the past twelve hours you have fulfilled the *repliegue*. Nicaragua is proud of you.' '¡Patria libre o morir!' rises the returning roar.

The *repliegue* being over, it remained to get back to Managua. I found an IFA, one of the towering East German military trucks that careen down the streets of Managua with their eighteen-year-old driver at the helm ('the most dangerous creature in Nicaragua,' it is widely said). Within its open cargo space sat some twenty marchers, mostly from the same militia brigade and in various states of somnolence. In another time and place they could have been a bunch of high school seniors returning from an all-night dance. A delicate girl with eye-shadow sitting next to me solemnly handed me a small slip of paper. On it were listed the chants and slogans for her group. They went as follows:

PUEBLO-EJÉRCITO UNIDAD ... GARANTÍA DE LA VICTORIA

AL PASO DE SANDINO . . . TIEMBLA EL IMPERIALISMO
AQUÍ ALLÁ . . . EL YANQUI MORIRÁ
EL PODER ES DEL PUEBLO . . . EL PODER ES SANDINISTA
DIRECCIÓN NACIONAL . . . ORDENA*

I am not a man of the crowd, and not a believer in the superior judgement of the young. I am uneasy about this recollection, as if it were a shadow within the dream of the *repliegue*. Were we swept along by the 'revolution', or by the 'national leadership' who 'ordered' the march, ordered the chants, put the water trucks in our path, sent the IFAs to pick us up? If the median age of the marchers was something like seventeen (it is said that the median age of Nicaragua is only sixteen, though nobody really knows, there being no good vital statistics), why should this vast collection of teenagers, many of whom must have been along for a lark or because of conformism, constitute a genuinely militant force? What was the girl going to do when the 82nd Airborne came down from the skies like rain on the *repliegue*? I remember seeing the fighter planes of the 'Fuerza Aérea Sandinista' at the Managua airport – a bunch of rusting Korean War vintage jets, their wings listing crazily into the tall grass; and the fleet of Soviet-made attack helicopters that flew overhead at the Sixth Anniversary celebration in 1985. They looked glorious and thrilled the crowd, and certainly would tip the balance even further against the inept and cowardly contra. But against the techno-wizardry of the US military? The roar of the massed celebrants that 19 July as they saw the helicopters pulled tears into my eyes. What was the point of all this; and why was I getting so sucked into it?

But I was in no mood for speculation or doubt when the IFA deposited me about half a kilometre from Pedro Joaquín's home that Saturday morning in the barrio 14 Septiembre. I hobbled back through the interlaced alleys and the dirt roads with potholes into which a vehicle could disappear and never be found again, across the open sluiceways that served to carry off rainwater but

* United people's army . . . guarantee of victory; at the step of Sandinism . . . imperialism trembles; here, there . . . the Yankee will die; this power is of the people . . . this power is Sandinista; the national leadership . . . orders you.

15

sometimes got sewage as well, and onto the little street of no name with monuments to other teenagers martyred against Somoza. Past the two Chevrolet Blazers parked in front, up the stairs, through the odd little red brick arch with tiles on top, and into the cramped house, scrubbed clean by the strong arms of Liliana. And there was Pedro, who had met another friend while I was wandering and had just returned himself, by bus.

'¿Qué pasó, hermano?' What happened, brother?

2

THE
CLINIC

THE NATIONAL PSYCHIATRIC HOSPITAL of Nicaragua lies behind an iron fence at the western edge of Managua, close to the Carretera Sur, local incarnation of the Pan-American highway. Just beyond the hospital the road rises sharply, passing between dome-like hills that once were volcanoes. On one side is the FSLN mountain, whose colossal white letters bearing the name of the reigning party can be seen from the airport at the opposite end of the city; while on the other, on a lower hill of no particular name, sits a heavily guarded palatial dwelling, said to be the finest site in all Managua. Once the home of Somoza's mistress, the palace is now occupied by the United States detachment in Nicaragua. There marines and Embassy personnel – and the other US insiders – relax and escape the hard conditions of Nicaraguan life. They play tennis, swim in the pool, enjoy the Budweisers and hamburgers flown in for their pleasure, and, it is said, gnash their teeth at having to look up to the hated letters on the mountain to the west.

The Embassy itself is conveniently located on the other side of the hospital, on a large compound, also heavily guarded, although in this case the security is mostly provided by a special detachment of the ever-solemn Sandinista police. Through a side entrance stream the Nicaraguan suppliants seeking visas or the US citizens with one problem or another. The main gate is for vehicles and ceremonial events befitting the peculiar circumstance of maintaining diplomatic relations while making war upon one's host. Among the ceremonies is the weekly vigil of US citizens in Nicaragua protesting the policies of their government. I had been to the first of these 7.30 a.m. exercises on Thanksgiving Day 1983, and attended religiously each Thursday during my visits to Nicaragua. This time the proximity of the Embassy to the hospital proved to be a real convenience, the two institutions being so close that the ever-present probability of an automobile breakdown scarcely mattered.

The psychiatric hospital also has a guard in front, less to keep patients in than to keep contras out. In fact, all medical settings in Nicaragua have guards posted, who check the papers and bags of those who enter. This is a response to the counter-revolutionary strategy of attacking health facilities in order to demoralize the population, thereby proving to them that 'communism' doesn't work. Thus there are communities in the north of Nicaragua who have not had medical care for four years. In the instance of the psychiatric hospital, however, there is no actual sense of danger and the behaviour of the guard is languid and perfunctory. And, it may be added, the place is already virtually demoralized to the limit.

It seems to me that neither the contagious nature of madness nor the shabby appearance of its physical plant explains the peculiarly melancholy aspect of the National Psychiatric Hospital of the Republic of Nicaragua. Every psychiatric facility is, after all, full of depressing madness, and I have seen many with a more disturbed range of patients that were more cheerful places. As for the appearance, that is never decisive, in my opinion, and is in any event as much an effect as a cause of a place's mood. I do not wish to suggest, however, that the hospital was not shabby. It most surely was. A haphazard collection of mottled white stucco buildings dating from the dictatorship in the thirties, and seemingly unpainted since. A few palm trees between the buildings and some ragged tufts of grass, but otherwise an expanse of dust. Inside, the wards are clean, open to the air and utterly without privacy. The poverty is appalling – there are no sheets, for example, on most of the beds – but the poverty almost everywhere in Nicaragua is appalling without being forlorn, and forlorn is the word that best describes the psychiatric hospital. Patients of course are usually eager to leave a psychiatric hospital. In this case, the desire was shared by the staff as well. I have never met the person who was not eager to get out of it.

No, that is not quite right. There was a woman, a resident psychiatrist, one of the new breed being trained in revolutionary Nicaragua. Carlota was her name, and she stood out from her peers by her age (she had just turned fifty) and her zeal, which was evangelical. Carlota was a Mother Teresa in the rough. She had come late to medicine, after bearing and raising nine children, and having been abandoned by her husband. This seemed to release her pent-up ambition. As only two children were still small, she was able to park them with her mother and, with the aid and encouragement of a Protestant minister, commence higher education and medical study in Brazil. When she returned, the revolution had triumphed, but its bureaucracy considered her too old to begin psychiatric training. She went back to Brazil to begin her psychiatric education and finally transferred back to Nicaragua.

Carlota was sympathetic to the revolution without being integrally part of it. She had a purely Christian view of the world, unencumbered by rationalist assumptions. There were times when Carlota seemed to be ranting, or even a trifle delirious, but she did her work reliably and kept away from the deep end. For her, mad people were *prójimos*, fellow-beings who had gone astray. In the expansive script she wrote in my notebook when I revealed my ignorance of the word, *prójimo* was connected with *tu semejante-tu hermano-tu vecino*: your likeness-your brother-your neighbour. There was no essential boundary for Carlota between us and the mad. She saw insane people as individuals before God, without any mediating social structure to form or deform them. They were the 'least of these' whom the Gospel of Matthew made equivalent to Jesus himself. The crazier and more dilapidated the patients, the more did Carlota want to be with them. And since the psychiatric hospital gathered into its bosom some of the craziest and most dilapidated people imaginable, Carlota was perfectly happy there.

I don't think any of the other professionals were, not really happy. Though they worked hard and loyally, they did so under a set of assumptions that kept them from enjoying the fruits of the revolution. Not so for Carlota. For Carlota, there was no basic

19

contradiction between her evangelical Christianity and the revolution. Even though she was not really a Sandinista, she came from the same root: that all people were *prójimos*, and, crucially, that they had the capacity to transcend themselves.

Religion, which comes before the modern world-view, and revolution, which presses beyond it, are united in opposing the current consensus about human nature. In the modern age, the ruling notion has been that there is no point in transcending ourselves. We are what we are, here and now. This cleared the way for what has been called the scientific study of human beings, one of whose outcomes has been medical psychiatry. And the sensible, efficient, rationally controlled citizen, who knows how to live within the boundaries of capitalist society, and even likes it, became the cultural ideal. Those who play by these rules are sane; the rest are lunatics or outcasts of another kind.

Being a lot older than all of this, Christianity is not burdened by the notion that our human essence is reasonable, since if it were – by established standards, at any rate – we would deny the divinity of Christ, and of ourselves. Revolution, too, is not burdened with this notion, since the established standards of sanity and rationality are of a world which has to be overcome precisely because it distorts the human essence.

The other professionals in the hospital, however, were practitioners of a much more rationalized and medicalized psychiatry, which separates the insane from the normal. For psychiatry, mad people have 'mental disorders', which are inside them and therefore not in society; and nobody is capable of transcendence. There are no *prójimos* for psychiatry, only reasonable citizens adapted to their society on one side of the line, and lunatics with disordered brain-wiring on the other, the difference to be determined by 'experts' with the aid of that tablet on which its laws are graven, the Diagnostic Manual, DSM-III. One cannot take DSM-III seriously, with its decision-trees for sorting out the mad from the sane, and hold onto a transcendent view of human beings. Diagnosing the human condition as if it were subject to the laws of bacterial infections is the essence of technocracy. Only the technical experts – the professionals – high above the common throng are permitted access to the secret knowledge; and what they do is supposed to be beyond mundane judgements of value. Hence their power. Wherever this malignant tome has cast its spell, psychiatrists are to be found ferreting out the mysterious essence of mental disorder, and putting people into boxes accordingly. And sad to say, the National Psychiatric Hospital of Nicaragua is one such place. It was locked into psychiatry, whence its forlornness, which is how poverty appears when it is not consciously bent upon transcending itself. No matter how seriously its professionals took the revolutionary ethos of 'Nicaragua Libre', their practice within medical psychiatry estranged them from the revolution.

It was bitter for me to see the practices I had been quarrelling with for years reproduced so faithfully, and in a setting I had come to in search of radical transformation. But technocratic professionalism is a powerful institution. This was how the Nicaraguan psychiatrists had been trained, and how they passed on their training to the next generation. The whole business is sharpened, too, by the heritage of colonialism. The psychiatrists of Nicaragua have the classical affliction of those who have been imperialized – dependency upon what has oppressed them.

Even under the dictatorship, Nicaragua was never well stocked with doctors, and such doctors it had could scarcely be expected to soil their hands with diseases of the poor. But for this very reason, they were more or less contented and adapted to their niche. Along came the revolution, trying to turn everything upside down. Suddenly doctors earned salaries in the range of the common people. The differential between wages at the top and the bottom of the social scale is now something of the order of a factor of three – not nearly enough for a self-respecting professional. More trying, perhaps, was the change in power, and the whole shift in priorities and value. I remember a conference at the hospital in León: the representatives of the health workers' union had as much authority and respect as the medical staff. Nothing of the sort would have ever taken place before the revolution, any more than it would take place in the United States. Many doctors accepted the new power given to those below with greater or lesser degrees of success, but many others could not. And for these, there have been temptations aplenty in neighbouring countries or the El Dorado called Miami, not to mention the active influence of Uncle Sam drawing them there. Sometimes it is not even the doctor, but the bored or frightened doctor's wife, insufficiently mollified by the heavy breathing of *Bodas de Odio*, the leading soap opera. There are many ways for a doctor to leave Nicaragua Libre, and many doctors who have left. I recall a conversation with some elderly women, who turned, as is so often the case, to the litany of their health woes. Greatest among the complaints was the departure of a number of their favourite physicians.

Such things are not good for the revolution, which has responded by trying to make life as agreeable as possible for the remaining doctors. Private practice in off-hours (a generously construed concept) is allowed; and medical authority is retained wherever possible. In practice this means a reinforcement of technocracy, since the one thing a doctor can call his own is expertise. Even so, the country is down to about half of its pre-revolutionary physician population. The gap is made up to a considerable extent by international aid, and the first cadre of doctors trained under the revolution has come through, but the scarcity is still severe. The Ministerio de Salud Mental recently had to make do with fourteen trained psychiatrists for a nation of almost three million people. The law of supply and demand has raised the value of their service inordinately, and the psychiatric hospital has become their technocratic stronghold.

Happily, the psychiatrists are awkward as country boys in ill-fitting suits with their technocracy; and some of their better qualities break through spontaneously in those moments that have not yet become professionalized. I loved to attend 'ward meetings' on the Female Ward. This ritual has been borrowed from First World psychiatry, where the typical ward meeting is a litany of complaints, whines and reminders of medical authority. In Nicaragua, however, everybody joins hands in a circle and introduces themselves to the applause of the others. Then the patients are asked to sing, which they do as the spirit moves them, again to applause. It is all very jolly and lasts for twenty minutes. Then the great stretches of dreary and empty time resume.

Although somewhat more technocratic than the ward meeting, rounds at the hospital are still jocular occasions, the staff coming into the cramped and dilapidated nursing station at their leisure, bantering freely and switching back and forth between a variety of inadequate seating contrivances. Patients wander in and out in their shapeless smocks, and no one minds. The doctor in charge has his place behind a desk, where he riffles through papers and periodically pontificates on one matter or another, now teaching, now pronouncing a decision about a case; but he is not a prepossessing figure and never in my experience made an overbearing display of authority.

He does not need to, because he is armed with DSM-III, the talisman of medical-psychiatric authority. In the national director's office in the Ministry of Health sits a stack of some twenty of the green glossy volumes of DSM-III, charitably donated to keep Nicaragua in the late twentieth century. Owing to difficulties in distribution, these copies have not yet reached Dr P, the attending psychiatrist for male patients. He still makes do with his much-thumbed stack of photo-offset copies, lying loose in the top drawer of his desk. As it does in North America, DSM-III keeps the doctor on top while sparing him the need to understand or even speak to the patient.

A case is presented, a very strange case indeed. A Chinese man lives alone in one of the desolate parts of Nicaragua's outback. He is cut off from his world. When he is well he travels considerable distances to do kitchen-work in restaurants. And when he is sick, as has occurred every few years for the last twenty, he locks himself in his hut, bars the door, and subsists on dogs, cats, rats and lizards, until someone comes to take him to the hospital, where after a few weeks he returns to normal. Now he has returned to normal, and he must be Diagnosed. No thought is given to speaking with this man, whom I in fact never see, and who seems to exist only for the purpose of having a number attached to his being. Instead Dr P pulls out his set of DSM-III from his drawer and proceeds to turn the pages one by one, calling out the diseases and seeing if there is any resonance between them and the facts of the case. No, it is not schizophrenia (280.xy) of this type or that, or cyclic affective disorder (209.yz), this type or that. Could it be this? No. Or that? No. It is like a game of Bingo. Finally, the facts of the case match something in the book to the satisfaction of the psychiatrist. Here it is: Recurrent Personality Disorder, Antisocial type (314.09). Ah, that explains everything. Bingo! The case is closed, and DSM-III goes back into the drawer.

When the medical psychiatrists are not trying to diagnose somebody, they spend most of their working time plying patients with drugs. I sat in one day as one of the senior doctors talked to a couple who had come all the way from Estelí, 120 kilometres over difficult roads, to consult with him about the anxiety attacks the woman was suffering. He barely heard them out, asking only the most perfunctory questions ('Is everything all right at home?' 'Yes.' 'Very well, do you have any other problems?'), after which he pulled out his pink prescription forms pinned together and separated by carbon paper, and supplied her with a two weeks' store of Valium to dull her pain. The session had lasted eight minutes. Off went the couple to the Huembes market bus terminal, which is on the other side of town, an hour's ride on atrocious Managua buses. There they could expect at least a four-hour trip to whatever was bothering them in Estelí.

On the other hand, when drugs are helpful, they may be unavailable. I brought down with me a sackful of psychiatric drugs culled from doctor's samples, dozens of different kinds of medicine, including some of the staple antipsychotic, Haldol, in injectable form. A very severely psychotic woman was admitted a few days later, as sick as anybody I have seen in the hospitals of the North. Being uncontrollable, she was tied into her bed, which she was soiling at a good clip. Of course, she would not admit anything into her mouth, giving rise to anxiety lest she collapse from dehydration in the stifling Managua heat. Someone wistfully remarked how nice it would be if they had any injectable tranquillizer, such as Haldol, to give her. I volunteered that I had brought some with me; and the next day the woman was up and around, mad as could be, but eating and out of immediate danger.

I think this was the most useful thing I did during my time at the psychiatric hospital. My imperfect Spanish made unassisted clinical work impossible, and no translator was available. Even had one been, my feeling of estrangement from the dominant medical model would have made work difficult. As if recognizing this, the senior psychiatric staff of the hospital gave me a wide berth. They were polite, and ritually suggested that we had to get together, but it was quite obvious they wanted little to do with me.

I can't blame my critical attitude toward medical psychiatry for all of the tension. A good deal of it is inherent wherever there has been colonialism and somebody from the formerly dominant power returns to be of help. Nicaragua was never a formal colony of the United States, but it might just as well have been, considering the degree and duration of the control exercised. The marks left by that grip are not going to fade away just because a revolution has shifted political power to those who had been dominated. The North-merican expert remains the colonizer, whether helping or not; while the Nicaraguans remain the colonized, even if they are nominally in command of their own institutions. Indeed, Rita, a psychologist friend who served as my translator when I worked outside the hospital, said that in her opinion the Nicaraguan revolutionaries are much less aware of their 'internal' colonization than they are of external threats to their autonomy. This is especially acute when transfers of technology take place.

'Advanced' technology is never neutral and can never be transmitted neutrally to peoples who have been victims of colonization. The problem is stickier with the *internacionalistas*, who come down full of benevolence and are received so joyfully, than it is with purely commercial or diplomatic contacts, where relations are formalized. Where there is affection, bad feeling is not supposed to intrude, and so the latent domination is buried deeper. Having once been the quintessential banana republic (even if it never grew that many bananas), Nicaragua was despised by, and despised itself in relation to, the great power to the North. The Northamerican still regards him/herself as higher, defined as being 'non-banana-republic', and the Nicaraguan regards him/herself as an inferior race, defined by the property, 'non-Northamerican'.

This barrier may be down in some places, but it is raised high whenever technology is concerned because technology is the real measure of Northern superiority. The Nicaraguan and the *inter-nacionalista* are supposed to identify with each other, but they can't here, and bad learning can be the result. The colonial complex leaves a residue of shame in the student, and since shame is mortification, a bit of hatred, too, which becomes self-hatred when the teacher has the mixed identity of a *compañero*, or comrade, and

25

a technocrat from the North. Unhappily, this may perpetuate the feeling of inferiority and interfere further with learning, making it superficial and formal. I think this may account in part for why instruments such as DSM-III are abused here even more than in the metropolis. And I think it may have something to do with why the bureaucracy in places like Nicaragua is so awful and why productivity is so low. At the least, this dilemma puts a special obligation on the teacher.

Because everything is more extreme in revolutionary Nicaragua, teaching there can be a confusing experience. I had some of the worst as well as some of the best moments of a fairly long teaching career during my stay. There was a series of lectures at the Association of Psychologists which seemed a splendid opportunity to let out my revolutionary approach to psychology. I decided to give it my best shot. After so many years of beating my head against the wall of professional smugness and indifference in the United States, here was an opportunity, I thought, to speak to kindred souls. I waxed eloquent for the first two lectures, on the need to overcome old-fashioned ways of thinking and to achieve a genuinely liberated approach to human behaviour and mental illness. Everybody listened attentively and asked questions diligently. All seemed well, though I should have been alerted by the facts that both sessions started about forty-five minutes late and fewer people were there for the second talk than for the first. On the third occasion, only two people showed up: the chairwoman, who was obliged to attend, and an effusively affectionate young woman who did her psychology in a bank and had missed the first two lectures. I had lost my audience. Why? One never knows, but it seems on reflection that I had contradicted the content of the talks with their form. Here I was, talking with great zeal about the need to break loose from colonial ways of thinking – and I was doing it imperially, as another missionary bringing enlightenment to the heathen. I wanted to give them strength and more power, but my way of doing it belied the intention, and as it was a terrible nuisance to get to these talks at the end of a workday, they saved themselves the trouble.

Then there was the clinic, to be exact, the Centro Nacional de Salud Mental para Niños, Adolescentes y Familias: 'Guadeloupe

Ruiz Ríos', named after another child-martyr of the liberation from Somoza. The clinic had been opened shortly before my arrival, with substantial fanfare and amid a growing sense of concern for the fate of children under the turbulent and often chaotic conditions of revolutionary life. Articles about child abuse and abandoned children began to appear in the press, along with calls for reform. One case in particular aroused the sympathy of the city: a boy had been found living almost like a 'wild child', or a Kaspar Hauser, right in the middle of a Managua barrio. The alarmed community called in some nuns, who went to the welfare authorities. Investigations were made, full-page stories appeared in the newspaper, and the newly formed Centro para Niños was called into the case.

As it turned out, this coincided with a considerable expansion in the clinic's capacities, owing to the generosity of the Italian government, which had sent material assistance, and the vigour of the Italian mental health community, perhaps the world's most progressive, which had sent half a dozen workers contracted for periods of up to four years. Yes, other countries – even the US's 'allies' – officially help Nicaragua. It is hard, as a Northamerican, to assimilate this perfectly rational fact, given the way we have become conditioned to regarding the Sandinistas, but it was there before me every time I chugged up the Carretera Sur to just before the Shell station (this being the standard direction one gave for getting to the clinic) and turned in through the big iron gate to the low and modern building that had been erected with charity money in the 1960s as a pavilion for psychiatric patients.

The clinic occupies a spectacular setting on the lip of a dead volcanic crater with a lagoon at the bottom, and as if in response, has a vaguely resort-like appearance, with a small reflecting pool in which the children could float model boats, and a large covered terrace which seemed to be a dance floor. The structure had lain fallow for years until the injection of Italian funds permitted its rehabilitation, and it was still being overhauled during the weeks I worked there. Someday, this would be a fancy, well-equipped and thoroughly modern establishment. Even now a capacious Toyota microbus, courtesy of Italy, stands outside to take the staff on home visits and to pick up patients, while behind the locked doors of a

27

closet sits many thousands of dollars-worth of medical technology, equipment for a photo darkroom and an elaborate video apparatus, to be eventually used for documentation and research.

For the present, however, there is no telephone to go with this impressive technology, which made the work rather inefficient; nor was there much food, either, because we were in Managua, and because somebody forgot to fill out the right form at the right time, so that even the meagre allotment given to institutions was not forthcoming. For several weeks lunch consisted of a scant portion of plain beans and rice, served with water. The kitchen was so embarrassed, it refused to ask for the meal coupons with which the clinic workers had been provided.

What the clinic did not lack was *esprit*, an eagerness to help and to learn. And although it was directed by a psychiatrist, the amiable and garrulous Dr Ayerdis, it was free of hierarchy and psycho-technocracy. In fact, it was the sort of place a revolutionary mental health centre is meant to be. And because I and the clinic staff got to know one another directly out of shared work, instead of as an alien expert from the North, teaching there was a joy – aided, it must be added, by the translation ability of Rita, whose grand-father's cousin, Blanca Arauz, married General Sandino, and whose father had been a career diplomat under Somoza, stationed in the United States, whence Rita's fluency in English.

As had many of her generation, Rita had broken with the ways of her parents, and affiliated herself with the Frente Sandinista de Liberación Nacional during the struggle to depose her father's boss. A year ago Rita finally returned to Nicaragua, with her thirteen-year-old daughter. The child informed me that her school in Managua, the Colegio de Centro América, an establishment of the Jesuits attended by the children of many of the local élite, is better and certainly more demanding than its counterpart in San Francisco. She would accompany us on my evening speaking engagements, books in hand, and find for herself a side-room where she could study while I held forth.

The clinic gathered to itself the loose and shattered ends of the lives of Nicaragua's children. I am sure only a tiny fraction of the child misery ever found its way there. Some had lives damaged by the war – not the direct casualties, which form a minority of war's calamities, but the vast and ramifying streams of pain that drain away from the zone of combat. There was M, for example, eight years of age. She had been visiting her two older brothers, who were on active militia duty, when the contra ambushed them. One brother fell before her eyes, and then the other, her darling, fell coming to the aid of the first. Worse, her father had proved wanting at this moment of crisis. He stood there, frozen, while his sons died and his wife and daughter watched in horror. A year has passed, and the family continues in torment, with mutual accusations and endless pain. M became mute, stopped going to school, made countless threats to take her own life and suffers from constant nightmares. She is recovering a little now, thanks in some measure to the clinic. She wants to live her own life, but she is needed to fill the empty spaces in the home and her family's logic of expiation and revenge.

Then there are those who have been wrecked by the ordinary passage of life, Pavel, for example, the boy who attracted all the attention in the press. He had become the clinic's star patient. Most of the staff became involved at one time or another in the puzzling and frustrating case of Pavel, and I was drawn in for frequent supervision, though I must confess I had little to add, since at bottom I didn't understand the case either. Still, I think it was reassuring to the workers to have me listen to the story and make periodic visits to the amazing place called Pavel's home.

Pavel was fourteen, and he lived with his mother in Altagracia, one of the poorer, but by no means the poorest, of Managua's barrios. Most Nicaraguan neighbourhoods are in descending orders of poverty from ramshackle and seedy, but almost all are clean and well-kept within their material limits. So it was with Altagracia, which is why Pavel's home so outraged the sensibilities of the community and drew their cry for help.

Freud said that dirt was matter in the wrong place. He meant this as the difference between the inside and outside of the body. Thus saliva in the mouth is clean, while as 'spit' it becomes filth. But 'wrong place' is also a strictly social judgement. What can be used, that is, incorporated into the social body, is still clean. What has been used, though it be the same physical substance, is dirt. Think of corn on the stalk, the same cob after people have finished eating the kernels. A dirty or dishevelled dwelling is measured less by the amount of physical substance lying about than by the capacity of that substance to become incorporated, to be made human. Thus a dirt floor in the poorest hovel can be as clean as an operating room – if it is cared for.

The house in which Pavel dwelt was not remarkably more impoverished than its surroundings. Though it was dreadfully poor, it was surrounded by poverty only marginally less severe. Nor was there a great deal of such matter as could be called 'dirt' there. In fact the house was practically bare and had a Spartan look such as could be incorporated into the best Japanese or Scandinavian design. For all that the house – if such a word could be used – was astoundingly dirty. The only image which comes to mind in describing it is that of an animal's pen: outside the realm of the human, outside the fabric of care. There was no dignity to be had in it, no self-respect it could confer on its inhabitant. And so it roused terror in the community.

Let me describe it a little more closely. The house of Pavel stood back about fifty feet from the street, beyond a stony yard with a few scraggly flowering trees. A stone washbasin such as one sees in almost all Nicaraguan homes stood midway in the yard, along with a spigot that constantly leaked, so that the ground became mud. The house was one room, fairly capacious, about twenty-five feet by fifteen, and it looked taller inside than one would have expected, perhaps because it was so empty. There was a smell, high-pitched and thin, the smell of wet dirt that had never seen the sun. The gloom was relieved by light entering through several holes in the wooden walls and tile roof, so that one could take in the contents of the dwelling at a glance. These consisted of a heap of what looked like garbage at one end, and at the other, a rickety chair and the skeleton of a brazier supporting a few bent pots and pans. Turning to the wall, one beheld first, a small plaster Virgin on a shelf, and next to it, a faded print of Jesus. It was the same image as I saw each day in my alcove at Pedro's house, and again, on a large billboard near the intersection of the Carretera Masaya and the Pista de la Resistencia, a sickly and sentimental Jesus, looking directly at me, as if to say, 'See how I suffer; you are responsible for this, but I will not blame you'. It was the *Corazón de Jesús*, a popular Spanish image, named because Christ's heart was shown illuminated through his skin and wrapped in thorns.

One did not see Pavel upon entering the room, but he was there, behind the heap of what appeared to be garbage. It was, I suppose, a bed, or had been before he made it into his redoubt. The spring had been folded and packed with newspapers, so that one could not see through it. This formed the rear portion of a makeshift wall, the front half being comprised of the two ends of the bed, overlapping like the scales of a fish. Other scraps of paper lay about, obscuring the design of the whole. The yellow-brown foam mattress, which could be described as rat-eaten if a rat could ever be induced to eat such a thing, lay with one end on the floor next to the front wall, the other raised on a box. On it the boy crouched, naked save for a pair of grey trousers, on knees and elbows, peering out of a hole in the bottom of the wall. There he spent his days, mute and alone, save for the periodic apparition of his mother and her occasional lovers. I did not see her the first two times I visited Pavel, but she was there on the third, accompanied by her youngest child, a three-year-old girl who was far and away the unhappiest youngster I ever saw in Nicaragua. Giuseppe, the therapist I was accompanying, is an extraordinarily warm person, but he can be gruff in manner. Trying to cheer up the little girl, he tweaked her playfully under the chin, whereupon she commenced to weep heartrendingly for five minutes while her mother stood by in a daze. At last her daughter's suffering seemed to register, and she picked up the child, who returned to her customary sullenness.

Though she was born in the cattle country of Chontales, Pavel's mother is as un-Nicaraguan in appearance as she is in manner of child-rearing. With her ice-blue eyes, blond hair and thin lips, she bears genetic witness to a long-gone Teutonic visitor. She differs also from the typical Nicaraguan in comportment. Nicaraguan women are characteristically modest, but Pavel's mother had something wanton about her and was kept from outright seductiveness only by her dreamy and rapt air. She was thin and wore a loose smock which hung open when she bent over, displaying her small, outwardly turned breasts. Poverty was the reason she advanced for the miserable condition of her son, that, and the voices which spoke to her at night of the evil that would befall him. But the Virgin and

her Son would save them – she gestured at the wall. Jesus died for
the suffering ones like her son, and he rose on the third day; so she
had faith they would be saved as well. As for the house, it was
deplorable, but what could one do, they were so poor? But the
holes – why were the roof and the walls coming apart; more, why
were they coming apart so rapidly, day by day? Was that God's
will? Well, no, it was Pavel's mother's will. She was demolishing
her house, piece by piece, beginning with the section next to her
stationary son. This gave him more light and air, but more rain as
well, and it did nothing, to say the least, to improve the decor.

Giuseppe, who was a brilliant and intuitive therapist, took his
cue from the mother's demolition. Pavel occupied a junction
between the human and non-human, and his own naked and fallen
condition was mirrored by that of his house. One had to feel,
moreover, that his benighted mother was expressing her wish to
destroy him by demolishing the house. Why not, then, reconstruct
the house, which would protect and dignify Pavel, reassure the
mother against her own destructiveness, and draw the community
together in a project to help the family? Giuseppe had once been a
student of architecture in Italy, and he delighted in making precise
architectural drawings of the new dwelling, complete with a little
window near the floor in one corner, should Pavel wish to remain in
his observant crouch.

He had also performed extensively in street theatre, and
conducted his therapy like a Punch and Judy show. We always
brought a bowl of clinic food for the boy, which Giuseppe would
present with grand gestures, as if it were room service at the Hotel
Intercontinental. Everything was acted out with extravagance,
rough-housing and feigned threats. Giuseppe would write with
crayon on the wall, pretend that he was going to dismantle Pavel's
little sanctuary, and tousle Pavel's matted black hair. The boy loved
it. He was a slender lad, with delicate but sensual features and
heavy-lidded eyes. One expected to see a withdrawn psychotic, but
except for the muteness and odd habitation, it was plain to see that
Pavel was very much in touch with what was going on around him,
and simply awaited the opportunity to rejoin the human race. On
an earlier occasion, he had done some drawings. Some were
gibberish, as if he were deliberately trying not to draw; while others

betrayed considerable artistic talent, inherited, no doubt, from his long-gone father, who was a painter. The image Pavel drew with the greatest facility was of a soldier in various postures of violent aggression. This accorded with his delight in Giuseppe's horseplay. Perhaps it indicated, too, his need to knit together his own psyche by turning his rage outward. Still, the violence contrasted sharply with Pavel's outward gentleness. But then, Nicaragua was full of gentle-looking fourteen-year-old boys slinging weapons, and the street corners had many monuments to martyrs of the same age or younger.

Pavel was a deeply disturbed youth, yet compared to some of the withdrawn, desperate and violent young people I had seen in the North, he seemed a model of sanity. And this was typical. I would go so far as to say there is substantially less madness in Nicaragua than in the United States, despite the ravages of war and all that is wrong with the Nicaraguan mental health system.

This is not to claim that there is not a lot of personal trouble in Nicaragua. The wildest supporters of the revolution would be hard put to deny this. In fact, the place is simply a mess. Centuries of oppression and poverty have become etched into the psyche, and the years of revolution and counter-revolution have torn up personal life as much as the economy. I seemed to be approached almost daily with entreaties to tend to somebody's neurosis; and talk of 'stress' and the heavy drinking which resulted was a favourite conversation piece. Pedro said that he had never seen so many people drinking on the *repliegue* as this year. The incidence of drunks makes driving at night an exquisite horror. The streets are mostly unmarked, with huge potholes and without lights; one's own headlight always seems feeble while oncoming headlights are blinding; and sidewalks are often absent. One never knows when some spectral figure will appear weaving across the path of one's vehicle, perhaps to his doom. I have been fortunate, but a woman I know, a nun, killed a drunken peasant who suddenly wandered into the path of her car on a country road near León. Such incidents abound. All of this is incontrovertible, even if it is hard to quantify or pin down exactly. One might think as well that the rate of serious mental illness – the major depressions, schizophrenias and

33

so forth – should be climbing, too. Nicaraguans should be going crazy in great waves, and the psychiatric hospital – which is, it must be added, the only facility in this country of close to three million inhabitants designed for severely disturbed people – should be bursting.

But such is not the case, and while it would not be correct to claim that Carlota will be going hungry for psychotic people to be with, the fact remains that the mad population of Nicaragua seems to be diminishing. At least the census of the psychiatric hospital is diminishing – from about 600 at the triumph of the revolution, to 280 during my first visit in 1983, to 170 today, July 1986. Now, of course, it is quite possible that mad people or their families, having heard how awful the psychiatric hospital is, decide not to go there for help, or short of this, find it impossible to get to the hospital, given the wretched state of Nicaraguan transportation. This may be so, but it is very unlikely, for three reasons. First, the hospital, despite many deficiencies, is in no sense a snake pit and enjoys, so far as I can tell, a reasonably good reputation, certainly above the threshold needed to choose it over putting up with the horrors of a psychosis. Everything I know tells me that for all the shabbiness, it offers care – which ultimately is a matter of human relationships – far superior to that of the dictatorship. Secondly, getting about Nicaragua may be awful now, yet access to the hospital cannot be worse than in the Somoza years, when the great bulk of the people were simply written off. What good was it to have functioning buses and ambulances if none of them could be afforded or went anywhere near one's home?

Finally – and this is the most compelling reason – I never had any sense, in a total of fifteen weeks spent in fairly close proximity to the Nicaraguan people, that there was very much smouldering or suppressed madness in them. Plenty of ordinary human folly, yes: jealousy, abandonment, malevolence, anxiety, 'attacks' of various sorts, all kinds of venalities. But major violence and madness, no. I am not disputing that some of this occurs: the mad people I saw in the hospital were as severely disturbed, and really quite similar to, the mad people I have seen over the years in the US. I am suggesting that the patient census in the hospital is a pretty good index of how much major emotional disorder there is in the Nicaraguan population, and that this is both substantially lower than in the United States, and dropping.

I worked for many years in a large medical-psychiatric complex in the Bronx, a borough whose population is approximately half of Nicaragua's. I do not have the exact figures before me, but there was never a time when we had less than a thousand mad patients locked up for one reason or another: roughly speaking, more than ten times the rate in Nicaragua. We know that the figures for psychiatric hospitalization in the United States have also been declining, thanks mostly to medications. However, this trend began well before 1979 (before which date also, the Nicaraguans began using the same medication); and as every visitor to a large American city can confirm, has mostly succeeded in pushing mad people, still quite deranged, onto the street, where they have become a major underclass of desperate and ruined individuals. All of this is missing from the streets of Managua, and from the texture of everyday life as well. The Psychiatric Emergency Room of a big city public hospital in the United States teems with bizarre and violent people; a few hours spent there can be shattering, a veritable voyage in hell. By contrast, the psychiatric emergency services in Managua are somnolent, and what one sees in them can usually be described as some variety or other of panic – the grinding, omnipresent anxiety of everyday life erupting out of control and literally knocking a person over.

A young woman shows up unannounced at the clinic. Her eyes are rolling, her shoulders, neck and throat are in a state of torsion, and she can barely utter a word. She doesn't know who she is or how this started. She responds a little to massage by Giuseppe, and is sent to the hospital. When I check the next day, I learn that she calmed down almost immediately, and was released.

Another time, passing the attending physician's office on the ward, my attention is caught by moans and cries. Inside, lying on the examining table, is a gasping and sweating middle-aged woman. She is a kitchen worker, who prepares the daily vats of *fresco* (fruit punch) and the rice and beans for the staff and patients. As she moans, 'Ayúdeme . . . no quiero ser paciente . . . quiero ayudar a mi pueblo . . . a mi hijo . . .' (Help me . . . I don't want to be a patient . . . I want to help my people . . . my son), I learn that

35

her only son was severely wounded a month ago by the contra, since when she has had frequent attacks of this sort. Her condition is complicated medically by hypertension, which by my impression is enormously common in this nation of poorly nourished, salt-consuming and constantly stressed people; and economically, by what another worker laconically refers to as 'no tiene reales', that is, she is broke. Seventy per cent of the people in a recent survey of Managua claimed they couldn't make ends meet, even with prices of staple goods frozen, bus fares virtually free, and so forth. She is one of them, except that by bursting out into an attack she qualifies for some medical relief. Along comes a resident physician, a cheerful fellow named Guillermo whom I have just seen kicking a soccer ball around with some of the female inpatients. Without bothering to admit her formally or write up the case in any way, he proceeds to give her an intravenous injection of 10 milligrams of Valium. Fifteen minutes later she is back in the kitchen, no longer a patient, and serving her people.

We read about shortened life span in the Third World. Add together a string of such insults, which are the lot of poor people everywhere, and it is easy to see how the statistic comes about. For Nicaragua, add again the effects of war, which always kills at least as much by pestilence as by bullets. There are persistent rumours of CIA-spread biological warfare in Nicaragua, but one doesn't need to invoke any special plots to see how the CIA-spread war brings disease and suffering to innocent people. For example, many of the drunks who get run over at night are in this category. Then there is malaria which, after having been almost eradicated, is now rising again. One thousand cases were reported in the first six months of 1986, an enormous jump, and some of them are of a deadly chloroquin-resistant variety. The reason for this is found in the classical havoc of war: less resources for insect control; inability to go out and use the resources, because of contra disruption; and, critically, massive displacement of populations. The deadly malaria, for example, has come from Honduras, borne by war-tossed Miskitu Indians, and has begun to afflict the region around Puerto Cabezas, on the Caribbean coast. I remember the paediatric malaria ward in the little Puerto Cabezas hospital. The only mosquito netting in that steamy town was deployed there, to prevent further spread of the malaria parasite, and the room was full of sad-eyed Indian children, their bellies swollen with the parasite and their parents rooted at their side. It is not only by blowing up trucks with land mines that one can terrorize a people.

Mostly, I think, the strain of their life makes many Nicaraguans torpid and inefficient. Instead of panicking, they become more relaxed and do less. Of all the numberless problems of Nicaragua, this slackness among the population caused the most grief to thoughtful people. I have seen some close to tears as they discussed it. What the contra does to interfere with production, or what the blockade does to deny the economy spare parts, harms Nicaragua greatly. But I doubt that it exceeds the damage from poor productivity. And however much this is rooted in the backward traditions and institutions of the country, it is the immediate result of the torpor that afflicts the average Nicaraguan worker, especially that portion who are in the revolution without being highly developed revolutionaries. And these are in the majority. There may be as many as 50–100,000 conscious Sandinistas: an impressive figure, especially when one considers that upon the triumph of the revolution there were probably no more than 1,500, but not the majority of the workforce, by any means. And the others – patriotic perhaps, not counter-revolutionaries, not even right-wing or bourgeois – comprise the body which does not move, whose watchwords resound through the offices and workplaces of Nicaragua: 'no hay' and 'no se encuentra' (there is none; he/she is not in).

BUREAUCRACY AT WORK

Everybody has their own Nicaraguan bureaucracy story. Here is mine, not the most outrageous, by any means, but representative. It is really two stories woven into one by the fact that they occurred on the same days – in fact, the days just before the *repliegue*.

I want to go to the Atlantic coast, and I want to visit the Berta Calderón's women's hospital to interview some doctors about the abortion crisis. I obtain a press pass through the agency of an influential friend, and try to pursue my goals.

First to the Atlantic coast: I use the same contact to get the press office of the Ejército Popular Sandinista, or EPS, or the army. There I meet Compañera June Mulligan, born of an Irish-Yankee father and a Nicaraguan mother, bilingual with a generic Northamerican accent sounding mostly like Tennessee or California, but all Sandinista and very cordial. Yes, it is very difficult to get to Puerto Cabezas, administrative centre of the war-torn and isolated province of Northern Zelaya, but she will smooth my path through the bureaucracy which issues internal visas to the region, the Immigration Bureau of the formidable Ministry of the Interior, or MINT. June tells me to call the next day, and she will tell me how to proceed. I do so, and get the familiar wail: 'La compañera no se encuentra.' '¿Por qué?' 'No sé.' 'Don't know . . . all right, I'll call back tomorrow.' Comes tomorrow and another 'no se encuentra', and tomorrow and tomorrow, for the next four days, after which I am finally told that the *compañera* is ill, and that I should try the next week. On Monday of the next week I call again and learn that she is no longer sick but still 'no se encuentra'. '¿Por qué?' 'En vacaciones.' Try in another week. This is too much, as my time in Nicaragua is growing short, so I resolve to plunge back into the maw of the EPS press office.

After a long wait, help appears, a tiny, cheerful woman in a green uniform named Reina. She makes a few calls and tells me to come back tomorrow, when I will be able to pick up a letter from a Captain Tiffer, which will clear my way through Immigration. This works, and the next morning I take the letter to Immigration, which happens to be at the other end of Managua. I find a bored-looking *compañera* in a uniform with lieutenant's stripes. She inspects the letter closely and informs me that it is no good. Why? Because it is not addressed properly; it has to be addressed specifically to Captain Morales, who is her superior, and then brought around to the other side of the building. Can't we just type in the name of Captain Morales above where it says Ministry of the Interior? There is room. That is for the army to decide.

I sense some inter-bureaucratic rivalry between these two most powerful Nicaraguan institutions, with the EPS slighting the MINT by not addressing the letter to an officer of rank equivalent to Captain Tiffer, and the MINT forcing the EPS to humble themselves by retyping the letter. Back at the EPS, Reina is as friendly as ever, but as for Captain Tiffer, well, it's 'no se encuentra ahorita'. Please come back in an hour. An hour later: so sorry, the Captain 'no se encuentra todavía'. Still . . . when will she return? 'No sé . . . tres horas tal vez . . . ¿por qué no regresa mañana?' This is too much. I decide to feign (not entirely) a tantrum. I won't wait three hours and I won't come back tomorrow. I must have the corrected letter now. Reina says she will see. Forty-five minutes later the letter, retyped and signed by Captain Tiffer, is in my hands.

Back across town, the Immigration office is closed for a two-hour lunch. I return at the end of the day, to find the place deserted. Eventually the bored lieutenant materializes at Window 11, approves my letter and sends me to the back of the building, where they make some more phone calls and send me back to Window 11, where the bored lieutenant calls again, fills out a form and hands it to me, saying that this is a form to get the form to go to Puerto Cabezas, and that I should come back in two days, as it takes at least 72 hours to process the permission. But 72 hours is three days, I helpfully point out. Don't worry, just come back in two days.

Which I do. Now the bored lieutenant recognizes me and with a little smile, takes my form to get the form and gives me the form to go to Puerto Cabezas. One problem: the place written on the form is not Puerto Cabezas but Bluefields, the other destination of note on the Atlantic coast. I point this out and the bored lieutenant actually looks embarrassed. She snaps to, takes a blank form out of her drawer, types it up for Puerto Cabezas, stamps it, signs it and hands it to me. This takes about thirty seconds, less time than it required to prepare the form to get the form that was going to take 72 hours.

All I have to do now is to arrange my air transportation to Puerto Cabezas, there being no other way to get there. This has to be done in person at the airport. I drag myself to the airport (getting lost on the way in the eastern barrios) and find the little building where domestic flights are arranged. This was locked, though I could see a substantial crowd inside. Eventually someone opened the door and I joined a huge line of people squabbling over obviously scarce reservations. I knew I was doomed, and so when I was told that there was nothing available on the day I wanted and that the next possibility – on standby, no less – was 8 July it came as no shock. But my immigration pass is only good until 3 July. Sorry, you'll have to go back to immigration and get a new one . . .

THE HOSPITAL

In between trips to the EPS and the MINT I also pursue my investigation of the abortion crisis in Nicaragua, and go to the Berta Calderón hospital to interview some of the doctors. I make my way to Administration, flash my press card and explain my purpose. The woman behind the desk is very friendly, but she tells me that regulations demand that all interviews be cleared through the Regional Office of the Ministry of Health, happily just across the street. I am told to go to 'Planificación', and eventually find my way through the maze to one of the offices, where I explain my case to the sleepy-looking secretary who tells me to wait, as the *compañera* is inside having a meeting. Time passes, half-an-hour, an hour, an hour-and-a-half. Is there nothing that can be done? At length the secretary rouses herself and interrupts the meeting. The *compañera* comes out of the office, frowns in my direction, says there is nothing she can do and that I should go back to the hospital, and walks out. Now the secretary becomes compassionate and calls a friend over for a consultation. Together they decide that perhaps I should go to another office in another building of the complex. The secretary even takes me there. This time I do not wait so long before going into the official; and this time the official says she can help me get to the hospital. But there is one little detail. It seems that the press pass is not quite enough of a credential. Before she can give me a letter clearing my way, I need to give her a letter, only a little one, a *cartita*, which I can obtain from the same press office which issued me my pass. Why? It is the regulation. But don't worry, says the official, smiling cooperatively, I will take all the information now so that when you return with the letter to get the letter, I will have the letter waiting for you. Please hurry back.

Back to the press office, on the other side of town. When I first came to Nicaragua in 1983 the press office was a cheerful, open and efficient place on the top floor of the Hotel Intercontinental. Since then it has moved twice, and is now attached to the Casa de

Gobierno, with a considerable degree of security and sluggish bureaucracy. One has to knock on a wooden window to attract the guard's attention, after which he searches pockets and bags, and collects everything of a technical nature, including camera and pocket-knife. I go through this routine once more and enter the antechamber of the press office, where I explain my case to the friendly and cooperative secretary. Why of course we will get you the letter to get the letter to get into the hospital. Just fill out this request form and come back in two days, as that is how long it takes.

Two days later I return and find the women primping and filing their nails. Ah yes, your request for the letter to get the letter. It seems we can do nothing. You see, in cases of this kind we need permission from the Ministry of Health before we can proceed. But they say they can do nothing until they get approval from the press office. I'm sorry, you'll have to go back to them . . .

And that seemed to be that. But it really wasn't over yet, and therein lies some of the essence of Nicaragua. For although I almost gave up and resigned myself to a stoic philosophy of life in the face of these two bureaucratic defeats, eventually I ended up going to Puerto Cabezas and having my interview in the hospital as well. I just found other channels, or rather, other people to help. I learned that life in Nicaragua moves in a cycle: sinking downward, and then, just when one thinks nothing can be done, coming back up. It fits the redemption myth, but there's nothing mysterious about it. The cycle is produced by miserable material conditions and the torpor, which drives things down on one side, and on the upward cusp, by the presence of a communal spirit, which brings somebody to the rescue. One is never alone in Nicaragua. Someone is always nearby, often watching through the night. Liberals from the North often take offence at the vigils posted in every community, and the power of the CDS (the Committees for the Defence of Sandinism). With our heightened idea of individuality, it is hard to comprehend the spirit which keeps people so close to each other. Of course, this is easier to take when one is in need, as so often occurs under the conditions of Nicaraguan life.

I think this is why there is so little madness there, and why the mental health system works so well, despite itself. For poor, broken-down Nicaragua has a communality that the rich nations once had and now have lost. Psychiatry is basically a substitute for this communal spirit, destroyed by the industrial revolution. Madness, which is a given existential possibility for human beings, grows when the primary bonds which hold people together in a community dissolve. In the industrial societies, psychiatry, like all the king's horses and all the king's men in the nursery rhyme about Humpty-Dumpty, cannot put the community together again. On the contrary, its medical technocracy only worsens matters. And so our streets are full of drugged fragments of human beings.

On the other hand, Nicaragua, like all 'backward' countries, had a stronger sense of community to begin with, and it has had a revolution as well, which builds a communal spirit through all the confusion and conflict. Revolution sharpens conflict with the propertied classes, whose screams are heard so loudly in the Northern media, but it binds together the majority at the bottom by giving them a sense of purpose and of being cared about. For the masses, joined by a common project, there is simply less aloneness. The hysterical kitchen worker who kept crying that she wanted to 'serve her people' was not mouthing an empty phrase. And the way Pavel's neighbourhood rallied round, the way the press called attention, and the way the clinic, spearheaded by Giuseppe, came to the rescue, was deeply moving. It is hard to imagine something of the sort happening to someone so wretchedly poor in an 'advanced' industrial society. Of course we have our charities, but these exist precisely because there is no popular, spontaneous and communal alternative. Without our experts, we do not take care of the 'least of these'. Nicaraguans do not have to be reminded to do so.

The pathetic Nicaraguan bureaucracy and their foolish application of psychiatric technocracy are of the same piece: clumsy imitations of the master. I do not know how or if they will solve their hideous problem with productivity, but it is an ironic relief to see psychiatry so ill-applied. Since it is so weak, less harm will be done, while the communal possibilities for treatment will be given more space to grow.

The man who supervises all this sits in a tiny office tucked away in the Ministry of Health, assisted by a secretary who takes half-an-hour to type a one-paragraph letter. His name is Mario Flores

Ortíz, and he is older by a whole generation than even the senior Sandinista leadership. Flores Ortíz is also the only Nicaraguan psychiatrist to have been a founder of a political party – the Nicaraguan Socialist Party, which means in fact, the Soviet-aligned communist party. He is also possibly the bravest psychiatrist I have known, having risked his life on a number of occasions defying the fascistic regimes of Nicaragua and El Salvador. The Socialist Party still exists as one of the parties to the so-called left of the FSLN, berating the government for its policy of a mixed economy; but Flores Ortíz left it sometime in the 1970s to join the more activist Sandinistas. There is no other psychiatrist of his stature in Nicaragua, and it is hard to see who can replace him. Unhappily, Flores Ortíz is not in good health, having suffered a crippling automobile accident four years ago that left him lame and partially deaf and blind. Still, he commands the system like an old lion (albeit one with a bald pate). He was the only intimidating person I met in Nicaragua. In part this was due to his manner of conversing, which combined a severe formality with the habit – we could never decide if it was simply a consequence of his injuries or a controlling ploy – of staring blankly at his interlocutor through his thick glasses. And in part it was my perception of Flores Ortíz as an organic, anti-psychoanalytic psychiatrist who probably never wanted the likes of me coming down and disapproving of his psychiatric system in the first place.

Then one day he showed up at one of my psychoanalytic seminars at the clinic. He was attentive, and though it remained plain that psychoanalysis was not his wavelength, I began to feel that we might be able to communicate. Shortly before I left he made it known that he wanted to see me. He had heard through his daughter, who was a psychologist at the clinic, that I had had some problems, and he wanted to hear them. I obliged, and found to my surprise that he shared many of my views. I should have expected that a seasoned and highly conscious revolutionary like Flores Ortíz was going to be sensitive to the persistence of colonialism. What I could not have known was how easy it would be to converse once the ice had been broken. We talked of many things besides the contradictions of mental health care: of Carlos Fonseca, guiding spirit of the FSLN, whom Flores Ortíz had known when the great revolutionary was just out of college; of Pedro Joaquín Chamorro, Somoza's liberal antagonist, whose murder by the dictator set off the last phase of the insurrection; of the bitterness of class struggle and the neuroses of war. At length the conversation turned to the ubiquity of stress in the population. Much is made of stress in the Nicaraguan people, said Flores Ortíz, but the concept is inadequate. It treats Man as a machine or a purely biological preparation. After all, stress is an education, too.

So is the revolution, I thought as I drove back to the clinic. Revolution, stress and education – different angles of the same thing. When I arrived Rita told me that I had just missed Pavel. He had come for the first time. They gave him a haircut.

3

SAN
PABLO
APÓSTOL

Comunidad de San Pablo
de los barrios orientales
ha sido luz y fermento
en todos los lugares.
Ser cristianos es compromiso
sacrificio y unidad
al luchar juntos con Cristo
por la paz y libertad.
Los miembros de San Pablo
nos sentimos muy dichosos
porque vamos de la mano
con los internacionalistas.
Los hermanos europeos
los latinoamericanos
lucharán todos unidos
con los centroamericanos.
No les digo 'adiós' hermanos
ni les digo 'hasta siempre';
porque 'el Nicaragua Libre'
seguirá siempre cantando.*

* The community of St Paul/of the eastern neighbourhoods/has been a light and a ferment/everywhere./To be a Christian is a commitment/of sacrifice and unity/to struggle together with Christ/for peace and liberty.

As members of St Paul/we feel very happy/because we are hand in hand/with the internationalists./Our European brothers/the Latin Americans/ will all struggle together united/ with Central Americans./ I don't tell them, 'goodbye, brothers'/ nor do I say, 'until whenever';/ because Free Nicaragua/ will keep on singing forever.

THE NAME of barrio 14 Septiembre commemorates the date in 1855 when the Nicaraguan people expelled William Walker, the first of many Northamericans to invade Central America. Otherwise one would have to call it a nondescript place. Until this trip to Nicaragua, I cannot recall hearing of this shapeless labyrinth and had no idea that it was the neighbourhood on my right as I neared the Ministerio de Salud on the infrequent expeditions to that institution. For 14 Septiembre looks much like other Managua neighbourhoods. It is about midway down on the scale of poverty, which means that there aren't too many slapped-together shacks and approximately half the streets are paved. The neighbourhood is stable, though not particularly old, and it is the site of the original Christian base community in Nicaragua (and the second in Latin America, after San Miguelito, in Panama), San Pablo Apóstol.

The 1960s were years of development for Nicaragua. Capital flowed, Managua grew, and in the north, an agricultural industry centred on cotton flourished. Great numbers of displaced peasants came to the capital, where they formed the nucleus of an urban proletariat. The eastern barrios, including 14 Septiembre, took their present shape. At first they were without a place of worship. This was nothing new, since the poor in Latin America were often denied parishes, simply through neglect. But the Catholic Church was also changing in the 1960s. Beginning with Pope John XXIII and the Second Vatican Council, an inexorable spirit of innovation moved the church from its stronghold among the upper classes toward the poor. In 1966, a young Spanish priest, Father José de la Jara, asked permission of his bishop to begin a pastoral project in the eastern barrios. Permission was granted, and the parish of San Pablo Apóstol was inaugurated on 21 June.

Twenty years later, the birthday of San Pablo Apóstol was celebrated with fanfares by a new Nicaragua it had helped bring into existence. The walls of the little church in the barrio of 14 Septiembre were covered with the images, more than fifty of them, of martyrs given by the community to the struggle against the dictator and the counter-revolution. And now there was not only a new society but a new church to celebrate. The great convocations of Medellín in 1968 and Puebla in 1979 had convulsed Latin American Catholicism; the theology of liberation had been born; and San Pablo had become part of this history and an expression of the new theology.

I wanted to learn more about the Church of the Poor – the manifestation of liberation theology in Nicaragua – and so I approached my friend, Peter Marchetti, to see if he could place me in one of the communities. Marchetti is a remarkable character in a land of remarkable characters, and one of the extraordinary Jesuits who work in Nicaragua. The Society of Jesus took a marked interest in the Sandinist Revolution from its first days, much to the irritation of the present Pope, who cannot abide revolutionary Nicaragua. Pope John Paul II wants liberation, but his idea of this is something which stops short of challenging the Catholic hierarchy. However, the Jesuits, at least the ones who flocked to Nicaragua, joyously embraced the great social experiment embodied in the Church of the Poor, even if this threatens the foundations of Catholic authority.

The dozen or so men who inhabit the Casa de los Jesuitas in the sedate middle-class neighbourhood of Altamira are a reminder that the Society of Jesus was very much the original 'vanguard party' of political intellectuals. The comparison might seem outrageous, given the image of the Bolsheviks as ruthless atheists and that of the piety of the Jesuits. But one man's religion is another's heresy; and the discipline, selflessness, and above all, consciousness of historical mission that link the followers of Lenin with those of Ignatius Loyola are at least as great as what has divided them. And in Sandinist Nicaragua, it seems there is not much that divides them at all. This may be difficult to swallow for people raised on a diet of rigid anticommunism and who have been trained to see all revolutions as East–West conflicts, or to believe that Marxist-Leninist revolutionaries are incapable of adapting and learning from experience. This is precisely why it is important for US citizens – who of all people have been most indoctrinated in anticommunism – to visit Nicaragua and see with their own eyes things such as the convergence between the FSLN and the radical church.

Among the residents of the Casa are Fernando Cardenal, recently defrocked Minister of Education and architect of the highly successful literacy campaign, and Xabier Gorostiaga, perhaps Nicaragua's leading political economist. And then there is Peter

Marchetti, Northamerican, PhD, expert in agrarian reform and social transformation, currently in charge of advanced studies at the University of Central America (also a Jesuit institution), and man in motion. Marchetti was not content to walk on the *repliegue*; he had to run it, in a special marathon race conducted on the hot and humid previous Sunday, and despite the fact that he had not previously run over six miles at a stretch. But if there is something to be done, some challenge to be met, Peter plunges in. And since there is so much to be done, he is literally all over the place, laughing at adversity and full of optimism. There is no one I know who so combines intellectual sophistication with closeness to the people and their hardships. In the same breath he will tell you of his intimate acquaintance with amoebic dysentery ('the water I drank was alive with them!') and the latest wrinkles in Marxist dependency theory.

Marchetti's exuberance makes him one of the hardest people to meet with in Nicaragua. 'Call me after 11.30 at night or before seven o'clock in the morning', he will say, but even then it is hard to find him. Until this visit, I had to piggy-back on some other engagement to see him. Once I sat in on a talk he gave to a visiting group of Methodists from Iowa; once I went with him on a wild jeep tour of the countryside to pay respects to a peasant who had lost his son to the contra, for whom Peter had said mass the year before – after all, one stays in touch in Nicaragua; and once I just missed him entirely. This year, however, I had the time to track him down. When one finally corners Peter, it becomes easy to see why he is such a phantom. Everything is so interesting to him, he is so passionate about Nicaragua and what he is doing there, that what was to have been a five-minute conversation effortlessly turns into an hour before we realize it, leaving him negative time for his next engagement. Of course my request is of interest to Peter. The Jesuits take great interest in the Church of the Poor. He promises to talk it over with some of his colleagues and get back to me.

Two days later, he is on the phone. 'Listen, I think I've found somebody. We can't have you in the countryside, because you have too many other projects in Managua, and anyhow, it would be too hard for you to follow what is going on there. But there's a man who is good at this sort of thing. He's a leader in his community, pretty sophisticated, and he can deal with broken Spanish. I've given him your number.'

PEDRO JOAQUÍN ROMERO

And that is how I met Pedro Joaquín Romero.

I knew things were going to work out well with Pedro Joaquín when he first called. The connection was more than usually atrocious, with a cackling static that sounded as if the bombing of Managua had begun, yet somehow we were able to make sense of each other's pulverized voices. 'You can't come right away? Fine, meet me at the Banco de Desarrollo in front of the Centro Comercial at noon. I will be driving a red Chevrolet.'

It was the Blazer, a vehicle made for Texans to cover or, I suppose, 'blaze', their range. In Nicaragua, one takes the car one gets; and Pedro Joaquín was fortunate enough not only to get a Blazer but to find another Blazer for parts as well. This was kept on permanent exhibition in front of his house, in an advanced state of decomposition, its naked axles on bricks and its windshield in his living-room. There was another car behind it, of an anonymous brand (though it may have started life a Mazda), so extensively had it been reworked. One could usually find the man who was reworking it, Roberto, underneath one or another of the vehicles, toiling away on his back and employing a fascinating set of tools drawn from all parts of the globe, some of them improvised.

Someone should write an ode to Nicaraguan car-mechanics. Roberto was one of a cadre of men who worked around, or with, or for, Pedro Joaquín. They would come occasionally for breakfast, to sample Liliana's entropic concoctions, or to chuck little Bayardo Arce under the chin as the infant sat gurgling, tied to his chair by a sheet. Or they would use the bathroom or take a shower, except for Tuesdays and Fridays, when the water was shut off. During the day they could generally be found working with Pedro Joaquín around the corner at his *empresa*, or enterprise: 'impresores unidos – impresos de calidad', according to the neat sign in front. Here business forms – invoices, bills, letterhead stationery, and so forth – were produced for Managuan enterprises, on antique hand-set linotype machines and out of huge rolls of paper that Pedro got whenever he could, and trimmed to size with a chain saw.

In both form and content of his work, therefore, Pedro Joaquín would have to be called a representative of private enterprise. He owned his own business, hired paid labourers, and made materials to help other privately owned enterprises realize their profits. There is nothing remarkable about this, needless to say, nor about the associated fact that Pedro was what one might call a pillar of his local church, even a deacon. Millions of small businessmen are just that. What makes him interesting from a social standpoint, however, is that the church in question is an exponent of liberation theology, and that Pedro is also what would have to be called – given the current coding – a committed communist. He is the kind of person Ronald Reagan warns us against, the kind who is supposed to be turning Nicaragua into a 'totalitarian dungeon'.

If one examines Pedro Joaquín's passport, one will find there stamps certifying visits to Cuba and the Soviet Union. (Once I suggested that he visit me in the United States; and he replied, quite accurately, I am afraid, 'I would never get a visa to travel in the US, given where I have been'.) In fact, Pedro did not just visit Cuba – he went to school there, sent for three months in 1982 by the Sandinista Army, in which he was then serving, to study political theory so that he could become the political officer of his battalion. One would have to say, then, that he was considered 'ideologically reliable', nor is there any indication that he has shifted his views since 1982. Pedro is not, however, a Sandinista 'militante', that is, one of that small number (a few thousand, I would guess) who work full-time (and I mean full-time) for the revolution in one capacity or another. The reason for this is not that he cares less for the revolution but that he cares more for his church, and does not want to be taken away from it by party work. In this regard, if one looks again at his passport, one will also find certification of visits to Spain, Belgium and Italy, each for some international function of the Church of the Poor and liberation theology.

Pedro Joaquín Romero was born forty-three years ago on a small farm in Chinandega, in the rich cotton-growing north-west of Nicaragua. He was the oldest of three brothers. As a boy Pedro picked bananas and worked in the cotton fields, and then came to

Managua in that great migration which created the social found-
ation of the base communities and the growth of the urban
proletariat. And a proletarian he became, learning the craft of
typography, joining the typographer's union and eventually
becoming its leader. In 1966, he joined Dr Mario Flores Ortíz'
Nicaraguan Socialist Party. This became his political home for the
next decade until the rising tide of Sandinist insurrection carried
him beyond the cautious and parliamentary approach of Soviet-
style communism. Like Flores Ortíz, Pedro Joaquín left the
socialists and allied himself with the FSLN. He was on the
barricades during the urban explosions of 1978 and 1979. During
the height of the insurrection, he sent his wife, Ligia, and infant son,
Joaquín Antonio, to relatives of hers in the outlying town of Tipitapa.
He remained in barrio 14 Septiembre as second-in-command of the
local forces of the FSLN, retreated with them on the first *repliegue*,
and returned in triumph for the victory of the revolution. Shortly
thereafter he opened his business, then joined the newly forming
Ejército Popular Sandinista, went to Cuba and returned to fight
against the counter-revolution in the mountains of the north.

And through all of this he was a *creyente*, a believer. There was
no moment of conversion for Pedro Joaquín; for as long as he can
remember he has been the devout one in his family. Nor was there
ever any sense of contradiction with his socialist politics. Yes, there
have been crises – a deep faith by necessity goes through crises – but
never a sense that religion and revolution didn't go together, neither
with the Socialist Party, which followed Moscow's line, nor,
certainly, the FSLN. On the contrary, the Sandinistas' approach to
religion has always been part of their appeal to Pedro Joaquín. The
following pronouncement of the FSLN in October 1980, could
have been written directly for him:

> Los Cristianos han sido parte integrante de nuestra historia
> revolucionaria, de nuestra lucha por un poder del pueblo y por la
> construcción de una nueva sociedad.
>
> En Nicaragua mostramos al mundo que se puede creer en dios
> y ser a la vez revolucionario consecuente, sin que haya con-
> tradicción entre ambas convicciones.*

* Christians have been an integral part of our revolutionary history, of our

51

Pedro joined the community of San Pablo Apóstol in 1968, and has remained since. Though there is no hierarchy in the community, it is plain that he commands a great deal of respect. I suppose this has something to do with being one of the more literate members of the parish. During the first meeting I attended, a letter from a priest in Spain – I believe it was from Father de la Jara, the founder, explaining why he could not attend the forthcoming birthday celebration – was passed around with a certain degree of discomfort, until it was handed to Pedro, who read it for the others.

Although we often respect a person who has accomplished much, it is not the accomplishment itself, nor any external sign, which is the source of this respect. Pedro was respected for his literacy and his Cuban training and perhaps because he kept learning, by reading into the small hours of the night. Or he could have been respected for his rock-like bearing, and his calm and deliberate way of speaking (which incidentally was a boon to me of the 'broken Spanish'). Or perhaps even because he owned a little business and was more established, therefore, than the others in the community; or because he had been a leader of the insurrection, or the political officer of his battalion; or for further accomplishments I knew not of. But all these things were, ultimately, only messengers for the inner state of being which causes one person to be deeply respected by others. Ultimately, Pedro Joaquín was respected because he respected himself, because he had a profound and serene sense of self-possession, and knew how to communicate this to others, through his deeds, but directly as well. I don't mean by this that Pedro was a self-confident person – though of course he was – and I don't mean that he had a lot of pride – which he did, though I never saw him take his pride to the point of arrogance. I think the best word in common speech to convey his inner state – though it's not a word that we can give a good definition for – is dignity. Yes, that

---

struggle for people's power, and for the construction of a new society.

In Nicaragua we will show the world that one can believe in God and be at the same time an effective revolutionary, without there being a contradiction between these convictions.

would be it: Pedro Joaquín Romero commanded respect because he was a person of immense dignity.

What was the source of this inviolable sense of dignity, and of Pedro's strength? I do not wish to portray him as a saint, or a flawless human being. I am quite sure there was a dark side to his nature, and his attitudes towards women left something to be desired. But the man gave the unmistakable impression of *having put himself together* – of being of a piece, inside and outside, lucidly and consciously. I think dignity is an outcome of the integration a person achieves, an integration between what is subjectively and objectively present, between what someone *is* and what he/she *does*. Far from being a condition of perfection, or innocence, dignity to me connotes a continuous active overcoming of one's self. That is why we can say it is a harmony which has been achieved – and why children cannot command dignity, beautiful and holy as they may be. For though children live, they have not yet lived. One has to have lived and suffered, known pain and failure and the loss of innocence, and overcome this in the practice of life, to achieve dignity. It is a condition of the inwardness that comes from experience.

If this is so, if, that is, the activity of one's life determines whether one is put together or not, then we have to say that in Pedro Joaquín's instance, since his practice was that of a Christian-Sandinista-communist, it was these three things which he had put together and made work. The specific circumstance of his life in a deeply religious culture which was undergoing a revolutionary rupture from the imperialism of the Yankee, this concrete conjunction in which he lived, provided these three possibilities for self-integration. He took them, embraced them consciously, and made them work in his life. I remember sitting with him at his table and hearing him say how privileged he felt being alive here and now, in poverty-stricken, agonized Nicaragua with the 'no hay agua' and the 'no hay' this and that, and the ever-present threat of annihilation – being alive and being part of this history, helping build a new church and a new society. It was his project, this Christian-Sandinista-communist way of being. He embraced it, overcame himself, and achieved dignity. Pedro Joaquín was a happy man.

I think this conclusion may be difficult for a reader in the United States to accept. We are accustomed to reading about all of the shortcomings of those social projects called 'communist' or 'Marxist-Leninist': the drawbacks of the party-state and the clumsiness of socialist economies; the cultural restrictions, excessive bureaucracy, limitations on the press, repression of dissent, and so on and on, down to the Soviet Gulag and Pol Pot. We can also find defences of these systems and of the way they have raised the lot of the poor, though this kind of argument is a lot harder to come by. In fact, a person raised in the United States – and, to a lesser but still real extent in the other Western democracies – is more or less assured of thinking the worst about anything connected with the word, 'communist' – if not as an absolute hell, then as a stunting of the 'free' development of human possibilities. The idea that a human being can embrace this hated doctrine, along with Roman Catholicism, and emerge as an integrated human being seems outlandish.

But we should try to escape becoming the prisoners of our received ideas. Reality seldom if ever conforms to what we have been told, and all too lazily accept. In any case, we are in no position here to make a judgement either on the larger merits of Marxism-Leninism or on the overall tendencies of the Sandinista regime in Nicaragua. Much about that is written elsewhere, and should be studied thoroughly and critically, as it is a matter of great importance. But I did not observe 'Marxism-Leninism', or the overall tendencies of anything. I lived in a man's house for a while and got to know him as somebody who identified himself with communism, Sandinism and the Church of the Poor, and who had developed an integrated and admirable character on this basis. Pedro Joaquín Romero obviously does not tell the whole story about Sandinist Nicaragua, but he is just as obviously an authentic part of it. This is his revolution, and he is its person.

Days in the Romero household began exceedingly early. I cannot say they began before the cock crowed, since there seemed to be a cock crowing throughout the night in the barrio, but they did begin well before the sun rose. Usually it was Liliana who started things off with her endless round of clotheswashing. This was a daily ritual, for even on the two waterless days of the week, the taps did not run dry until 6.00 a.m., which gave Liliana an hour-and-a-half lead on the water department, plenty of time to wash the sheets and her baby's diapers, and to fill the half-dozen or so large plastic buckets within which the day's supply was contained. Since every household did this, and since it seemed that at least as much water was gathered in advance as would have been used normally – plastic containers being one of the few items in reasonable supply – it was hard to see how the water shortage was being alleviated.

I am an early riser anyway, and it was good to awaken in the pre-dawn coolness to the sloshing of water in the basin, the slap of clothes against corrugated stone, and the soft cries of Bayardo Arce, an exceedingly docile, even phlegmatic, infant. It was good, too, to contemplate a stretch of four hours before having to try and start the car – time to read, write in my journal, tend to personal matters, and chat with the family. Viewed from long range, the revolution is a hectic, turbulent, at times chaotic process, especially in comparison with the stability of our society. Up close, however, everyday life unwinds serenely. For all of the privations and irritations, there is a grace about it, particularly in the early morning. It was even cool enough then to go jogging. I must have cut a strange figure, a gringo in his New Balance running shoes, picking his way along the hard-packed and undulating paths of barrio 14 Septiembre, past the already-forming lines of stolid women waiting for their provisions at the local food dispensary.

Sometimes the awakening was less pleasant. Ligia, the *dueña* of the household, was a schoolteacher and also what one might call an early-morning person. That is to say, she was often abed by eight in the evening and up at four in the morning. This was no problem, except on those days when she had to do some preparation for school, which she chose to type. Now the Romero typewriter was a gigantic thing, a veritable Big Bertha of a writing machine. Each striking of the key sounded like gunfire. I should point out that Casa Romero was not a house on the grand scale. The family slept upstairs, in an addition built by Pedro four years ago. There was a room downstairs which had been the master bedroom and was occupied at the time of my arrival by another house-guest, a Salvadorean exile named Ramón. This left me an alcove next to the kitchen, which was the room where most of the activities, including

55

Ligia's matutinal typing, happened. I had there an ancient army cot, which was always threatening to fold on me and once did, and several chairs on which I could arrange my little fan, clip-on lamp and other amenities.

The alcove was also the site of Pedro's substantial library, which he arranged by subject-matter. There were books on sociology and religion, Spanish translations of the Russian classics, a Spanish-language *Time-Life* nature series, and a number of tomes on accounting and law. All in all, an impressive collection – and the more so when compared to what is available in bookstores and public libraries. Libraries in Nicaragua are like the supermarkets: cursed by empty shelf-space and forced to resort to expedients in filling them which almost makes things worse. Thus, the average supermarket, vitiated by economic misery and strangled by the embargo, imposed by Reagan in May 1985, will contain whole aisles full of nothing but glasses, all the same size and overpriced; while the periodical reading-room of the University of Central America covers the nudity of its shelves with back copies of catalogues from US publishers. Some of my saddest moments in Nicaragua were spent in contemplating this horrid scarcity, in a nation hungry to learn. It was gratifying, then, to see Pedro's full larder of books. Perhaps they even deadened the clacking sound from Ligia's typewriter.

The sound must have been awful, though, because it drove Ramón from the house, for all the fastness of his room. His *compañera* from Holland – where Ramón had lived for six years – had just arrived, which perhaps contributed to his sensitivity. Ramón complained loudly, but to no avail. Pedro stood up for his wife, and Ligia was not about to change her ways. Casa Romero, for all the scantiness of its facilities, had been the guest house of many internationalist visitors, including the Brazilian radical bishop and poet, Pedro Casaldaliga. Their names and grateful comments adorned a guest book proudly displayed by Pedro and Ligia. The Romeros were veteran hosts, who had a carefully worked-out code of relations with visitors. So Ramón and Wilma left, and I inherited his room. I was glad for this but sorry to see them go. There is a kind of instant cameraderie among the internationalists, bonded together by common affection for Nicaragua, the sharing in its siege and the constant drama of its travail, and the mutual relief from the alienation felt at home. 'Here I feel free ... I can say what I please,' Ramón had expostulated one evening after returning from a brief visit to Costa Rica, a country which preens itself on its democratic tradition and freedoms. It had an ironic ring of repressed freedom of speech. A great deal depends, however, on whose ox is gored. In any case, the new room was a considerably more substantial domicile. And Ligia's work schedule must have changed, for I heard no more of the typewriter thereafter.

Pedro's two younger brothers also lived in Managua. One was said to be a 'militant', that is, a full-scale party member, totally involved in the revolution. This conjured up images of a fiery soul, swathed in red and black, and blazing with political ardour. The other was politically different. He was not a Sandinista at all, but a member of one of the liberal opposition parties, the Partido Popular Social Cristiano, or PPSC, i.e., Christian Democracy. One evening Pedro invited me along for a visit to his brother in the PPSC. I was otherwise engaged and had to decline. However, a week later, he said that his other brother, the militant, was coming to his house for dinner, and invited me again to join them. I accepted with pleasure, intrigued by the idea of spending an evening with a Sandinista militant – by implication, more militant than Pedro himself.

It was clear that Pedro and Ligia took this visit seriously. In the morning, the Blazer's windshield was removed from the living-room, along with a very large pile of what appeared to be wrapping-paper, presumably associated with Pedro's business. Some new bookcases were lacquered and installed, an orange Chinese paper lamp was hung from the ceiling, and the house was given a spotless going over by the indefatigable Liliana. After working all day, cleaning and preparing food, she retired and was seen no more. Evidently a person of her lowly station was not fit to be seen with Pedro's brother.

The brother was supposed to arrive at seven, which in Nicaragua means sometime after half-past eight. At a quarter to nine, a new Toyota Corolla, sign of status and/or wealth, pulled up to the door and discharged a small, pudgy man, his wife, another woman whose identity I never determined, and two boys a little older than Joaquín Antonio. All of these people were clothed in garments of the middle class, in sharp contrast to Pedro, who kept to his regulation jeans and T-shirt. The brother, who was introduced to me as Luis, was wearing a fine coffee-coloured *guayabera,* or shirt-jacket, and a pair of brown pressed trousers of some expensive material. His wife was a slender, sharp-looking woman who doted on him throughout the evening and made sure that his cup was full. I never heard her say anything, because as soon as everybody was introduced and had properly hugged one another, the women retired to the kitchen, where they gossiped and laughed, and from which they only emerged to keep the menfolk served. The men, meanwhile, settled down for some serious talk, while the boys, after thrashing about for a bit, yawned expansively and fell asleep on the couch and floor.

We talked man-talk, or rather Pedro and Luis chatted, while I tried to make sense of what they were saying and interjected a few comments every so often to prove that I was awake. Luis dominated the conversation, pontificating in a humourless mono-tone about the state of the world and the economy, and who had the real power in the FSLN's National Directorate. This wasn't quite what I expected from an FSLN militant, but he seemed fairly authoritative, and I was reluctant to make any definitive judgement given my imperfect grasp of Spanish. After about ten minutes, there was a knock, and another couple entered. To my surprise, it was the third brother, Manuel, and wife. As he was dressed even more flashily than Luis and, though pleasant, seemed to have little to say, I assumed he was the brother from the PPSC, especially as his wife could have just stepped off the plane from Miami.

I was resigning myself to being completely out of the conversation, until Pedro mentioned in passing to Luis that I was a physician from New York. Suddenly Luis began to display a notable interest in me. How much money did professionals and university professors in the United States earn? Was it easy to switch jobs and move around? Northamerican cities were wonderful, weren't they? He had only been there once, but the impression had not faded. The shops, the libraries, the general advance of life – all stood out. This only confused me further. The bearing of the man, his toadying to gringo civilization, indeed, his thinly veiled desire to relocate in the United States – none of this was the least consistent with the persona of an FSLN militant. I communicated as much to Pedro after the party had broken up, mercifully early. Oh, he replied, you are mistaken; Luis is with the PPSC, and Manuel is the militant. Luis is ten years younger; he grew up differently and always had his eye on the middle class. But Manuel . . . he doesn't strike one as a militant, either. Well, he is an economist and works in the Ministry of Finance. His speciality is numbers, and he struggles to keep Nicaragua solvent, which is to say, acceptable to the world market.

So they were different, and my categories weren't far off, even though I used them the wrong way. The man from the PPSC acted the way one would have expected a man from a Christian Democratic position to act, but where did that leave the 'militant'? It seemed that although Pedro and Manuel were united politically on the opposite side from Luis, in some fundamental way the two younger brothers had more in common with each other than either did with the older. Class was part of it, as the scrambling to bring the house up to scratch revealed. It was more than an economic matter, though. Neither of the younger brothers had the expanse of Pedro's soul, or his clarity, compassion and depth. For Luis and Manuel, despite their political difference, were each of them a technocrat. They were modernizers, the disenchanters of the world, toilers on the near side of Nicaragua, the side which remained attached to the world system. In the context of barrio 14 Septiembre and the community of San Pablo Apóstol, one would have to say that they lacked 'spirit'.

THE SAN PABLO COMMUNITY

When I came to barrio 14 Septiembre, I had no clear idea of what 'community' meant in the phrase, 'Christian Base Community'. I am sure it differs from one place to another. In San Pablo, the community was there, but it was not compact, and encompassed no special place in the barrio beyond the little chapel where people met and prayed. The community existed more in time than in space; it was a zone of living history made by its members, rather than a settlement. And it was small. I think there were about one hundred people from 14 Septiembre in San Pablo, which is a tiny minority of the barrio. Other eastern barrios had their contingent as well, which were of the same scale. In fact, one would be greatly mistaken if one thought of the Church of the Poor as a mass movement, either in the eastern barrios or in Nicaragua as a whole. Its importance has to be measured more in terms of what it represents and where it is heading than by the number of adherents, which is, I should think, less now than in, say, 1978. The revolution drove a lot of conservative people out of the base communities and has distracted a good number of others. But the greatest obstacle to the growth of the Church of the Poor is the well-organized Catholic hierarchy of Nicaragua, led by Cardinal Obando y Bravo and supported by the immense authority of the Pope. An image of Obando or John Paul II is the surest emblem of an anti-Sandinist home or business establishment in Managua; and even those who do not join in the hierarchy's opposition to the Sandinistas are readily inhibited from going over to the People's Church when it is so clear that the Cardinal and the Pope do not at all approve. For all this, the Church of the Poor seems to have turned a corner in its growth, with six new parishes in the last two years. On separate occasions, Pedro Joaquín and Peter Marchetti each told me that the period of post-revolutionary confusion and retrenchment seems to have been put behind, and that the liberation church is now moving confidently forward.

It would have been hard to persuade me of this fact as I accompanied Pedro to my first evening meeting of the community. The little church of San Pablo is not what would be called an inspiring place. Built of cinder blocks and with virtually no decoration, it looks particularly shabby in the dim blue light cast by its fluorescent lamps. About a dozen people were already gathered on execrably uncomfortable wooden folding chairs when we arrived. They were an unprepossessing lot, mostly middle-aged and careworn. My first thought upon seeing them was that their belief must be a consolation for the rigours and pain of their lives and the approach of death: religion as the heart of a heartless world. It turned out that with one exception, they had all been with the community for more than fifteen years, which is a testimonial to the stability of barrio 14 Septiembre, and also, perhaps, to a lack of new growth in San Pablo. The exception was Theo, a Dutch priest who had been expelled successively from Chile and Brazil. He was tall, thin and very blond. Theo had given up on doing anything in the institutional church, and wanted to live now simply by sharing the lot of the people. He supported himself by hawking the party newspaper, *Barricada*, on the streets.

Religious folk of all kinds flocked to Nicaragua in the wake of the revolution. And they still keep coming, mostly to visit but also in goodly numbers to stay and work. Every Thursday the demonstrations in front of the United States Embassy would be graced by one or more religious tours from the American heartland.

Then there were those whose commitment led them to stay on as part of the revolution. These were a different breed. Some, like Theo, came to seek holy innocence among the poor, or as George, who has been a Professor of Theology at a midwestern Methodist university told me, 'to get the rich out of me'; but the majority have been of an active, missionary spirit. Christian soldiers, I suppose one could call them. Marchetti was an example of this type, and there were numerous other Northamericans like him, Protestants as well as Catholics who have given themselves to Nicaragua. I often wish that our citizens, their minds fogged by anti-Sandinista propaganda, could meet some of these Christians. Marchetti is perhaps too much of an ideologue to be convincing to the average Northamerican. I defy anybody, however, to meet Howard Hiner and still retain stereotypes about the revolution.

With the proper beard, Hiner would probably win an Abraham Lincoln look-alike contest. I do not understand how the US Air Force squeezed his 6'6" frame into the cockpit of a jet fighter-bomber during the Korean War, or how he could see over his knees once in place, but he more than managed. Hiner, an all-out red-blooded patriot from Idaho, flew over fifty missions in North Korea, and he can describe the sensations of a dive-bombing run – including the times he almost didn't pull up quickly enough – in a way that brings a listener to the edge of his chair. After the war Hiner went back to Idaho and became an executive with the Georgia-Pacific lumber corporation, and a small-town Republican booster, in other words, absolutely the last person on earth one would expect to see dedicated to the cause of the Sandinistas. As he has said, 'Not many years ago I was totally committed to the official line of thinking about any country which our government chose to call communistic.'

But Howard Hiner was also a religious Methodist, and he and his wife, Peggy, felt a spiritual poverty in their lives. He continues (in a document presented to the United Methodist Council of Bishops to defend himself and the other Methodist missionaries in Nicaragua against charges by the right-wing Institute for Religion and Democracy):

> there was a crack in this rather narrow world – my membership in the United Methodist Church. So long and heated discussions took place with a variety of Methodist ministers that came to pastor our small church. They brought a broader concept of the love and grace of our Lord than I really wanted to admit – let alone accept.

Eventually the Hiners had a kind of conversion, renounced their corporate life and became missionaries. They spent years in Bolivia, Chile (where Hiner saw the Allende regime toppled through the machinations of the CIA), and Somalia. Three years ago they came to Nicaragua, where the erstwhile lumber executive now works as a forester, helping to restore woodlands destroyed by centuries of pillage.

Hiner has a very clear conception of how he has changed. It is a question of 'where one stands', that is, of how one actually lives. His lived world has now broadened, and so, correspondingly, has his view of it. He compares himself to the doubting disciple, Thomas.

> A few days after Easter, the disciple Thomas from 'where he stood' could not grasp the passion of the Cross and the resurrection. He needed a hands-on experience! Like Thomas I too needed a personal experience. I needed to travel to Latin America and see the sores, touch with my fingers the scars and place my hands on the wounds of the Latin American society – Christ crucified. But equally important, to experience the resurrection in the hope and faith of many, many Latin Christians. [His faith has given Hiner a global perspective.]

Thirty-six years ago I joined the USAF as an act of national patriotism. Today, I am challenged and called in my pilgrimage of faith to a much deeper form of patriotism and loyalty. A patriotism not confined to the ideological blinders of the 'isms', but calling our country to a higher road of international relationships. Our country needs to be reconciled to the God of justice and peace.

Hiner may have transcended the mentality of the Air Force, but he has retained enough to be quite aware of what a United States invasion would mean, and of how thoroughly the US war machine is geared up for it. Everyone I knew was conscious of the threat, but nobody seemed to feel it as keenly as Howard Hiner, or worked more diligently to keep it from materializing. He has a precise idea of which hills would be taken by the paratroopers, and of how the city would be shelled from them. And if the invasion comes? 'I'll hide out for about forty-eight hours, because that's when the worst massacres will take place – as in Chile – but then I'll come out again and keep struggling. I belong here.'

All of the internationalists in Nicaragua, secular and religious alike, have their particular reasons for being there. And all of these reasons are variations on one great theme. For centuries, the alienated intellectuals of Europe and North America have been looking for 'the people', in one incarnation or another. Ever since Western colonialism gained a world and lost its soul in the doing, there have been those who have gone to find that soul in the South, in the dark, in the ones who have been oppressed. The voyagers have included saints and devils, geniuses and fools. Some have been selfless and others self-obsessed. Taking their guilt and pride with them, they looked for themselves as they looked for the Other. They came to seek a history and ended by making it, sometimes well, sometimes destructively. For every Howard Hiner there has been a Kurtz of Conrad's *Heart of Darkness*, or an Ugly American.

Squirming in my chair on the first evening in San Pablo, the ambiguity of my own situation came home to me. I was not only a Northamerican: I was not even a Christian. It seemed there was no place for me, certainly not in this dingy church, and perhaps not in Nicaragua as a whole. I had been advised to stay at home, to cultivate my gardens. The struggle, I had been told, is in the US: beware of 'third worldism', recognize that Nicaragua is either a hopeless case, or full of violence, or, in any event, needs to be left alone. All this had been told to me by well-wishers and not-so-well-wishers; and the grain or two of truth in it came home to me as I sat waiting to be introduced . . . to whom? To these strangers from another class, race, nationality. No *prójimos-vecinos-semejantes-hermanos* these – and no *compañeros*, either: only Others before me.

But then the meeting got underway, introductions were made, letters were read, some passages from the Gospels discussed, as was the forthcoming birthday celebration. And I was made to feel welcome. It was this, rather than actually knowing very much about the community, that got me over my sense of strangeness. In fact, I can't say I ever got to know any of the 'people' really well, the way I know any one of hundreds of individuals at home. Language, shyness, lack of time, residual racism, classism, some 'ism' or another, got in the way. It comes down to the simple fact: this is not my home; I am looking for something here, in them, and this makes them Other. But I did get to know them a little, and then something wonderful happened – perhaps because knowing some-one means accepting their differentness, preserving them as they are, and also being able to take from them, and perhaps give in return. I don't know that I gave anything, except the encourage-ment that comes from establishing that there was one more gringo who wasn't a *yanqui* in their world. But I got so much, because to know these people a little is to feel their love. There is a beauty, a generosity, a vitality, in the poor of Nicaragua that speaks through the barrier. Just in themselves – and only them: sooner will the camel pass through the eye of a needle than a rich man have such virtue. The middle classes, best and worst alike, have lost it, have become desiccated in their possessing. It may be the lost part of myself I seek – that *sencillez*, that simple directness of the poor of Central America, that closeness to the source of things. But is it wrong if they have it, and give it freely, so that they are not lessened in the giving? Should one refuse this bounty?

Revolution is always about undoing the relations of class, of raising the low and bringing the high downward. From this perspective, the hostility of the Nicaraguan bourgeoisie, who have retained their wealth but lost their power, is understandable – as is, of course, that of the United States government. In a stable society, this polarization is kept intact, but once revolution happens, tensions between high and low spread everywhere. In Nicaragua, a nation of great piety, the struggle is transferred acutely to the church, the hierarchy standing for the disempowered rich and the people's church for the newly empowered poor.

But the poor are, needless to add, still poor, and in absolute economic terms they may even be worse off now than before the revolution. There is another reflection of the struggle, then, within the People's Church itself. Even here, there was stratification and one heard grumblings about priests who only talked of being with the poor, while they lived lives of the élite. Or the dichotomy would be played out in terms of native versus foreign. The People's Church has attracted a great deal of international attention. Radical clerics from all over the world have flocked to Nicaragua, to live and work; and thousands of progressive religious Northamericans have visited Nicaragua and returned to say no to Reagan. They come, as I did, to see the People's Church, which they often experience in the presence of Father Uriel Molina and the church of Sta María de los Ángeles in barrio Rigüero, not far from 14 Septiembre. Molina has perhaps done more than any other Nicaraguan to gain support for the revolution in the United States; and it is no wonder at all that the established church is trying to kick him out of the country. I had been to the services in barrio Rigüero a number of times, and had been enormously moved; indeed, it was Sta María de los Ángeles which more than anything else led me to San Pablo.

One would have to be made of stone not to be moved by the church in Rigüero, with its brilliant murals, passionate songs, and the Word as transmitted through Molina. Religion is much closer to theatre than we realize; and Molina's services are high dramatic art. He has achieved a ritualization that binds together the pain and dignity of the Nicaraguan people with the compassion of progress-ive Northamericans in a completely authentic way. On a recent visit, the service included the testimony of a Salvadorean priest on the ordeal of his parishioners who suffer the bombs sent by the United States. The power failed after a few minutes – scarcely an unusual occurrence – and we heard the remainder of his testimony in darkness. The lights resumed and Molina delivered a sermon in which Nicaragua was compared with Job (which I heard as 'Hub', causing me to miss a good deal of the literal significance). Then there was music, culminating in Molina's *pièce de résistance*, the singing of 'We shall overcome' by the Northamericans, encircling the altar, arms on shoulders. After the benediction, everyone hugged and wished each other peace. I found myself saying 'Paz' with scarcely any self-consciousness, as I clutched burly blond Los Angelenos and old Nicaraguan women so thin I thought I would lose them in my arms.

I say this because I am not given to casual displays of physical affection, and have always been made uncomfortable, and at times downright resentful, by the instant intimacy of 'New Age' culture. To me, these are based on the self-deception that true closeness between people can be attained without sharing an existential truth. People are hungry for such an existential truth, but the shallow engagement of our therapeutic culture excludes it in advance, and worse, allows people to kid themselves that they have encountered some deeper reality when all that has happened is the mobilization of a feeling. We live in a society designed to convince people that no fundamental change is possible, in accordance with which feelings and subjective states are made to seem the ultimate reality. I am not at all sure of what 'ultimate reality' may be, but I am reasonably convinced nonetheless that we are closer to it when we confront the historical world in all its suffering and struggle, than when we tend to our feelings and 'interpersonal relations' and play the various games of pop psychology. That, I suppose, is one reason I like to be in Nicaragua, and in places like Sta María de los Ángeles within Nicaragua. For here one is surrounded by symbols of heroism and martyrdom, gathered up in a sacrament where the blood of the eucharist and that of the victims of imperialism commingle, and conscious at every moment that the two cultures who have been the protagonists of this drama are present before each other. Existential truth is in the fabric of the moment, and so, therefore, is intimacy. Anything else would be unauthentic.

But this meant, of course, that Molina's church had to direct itself outward, to an international audience. It had to reflect the tastes, needs, and, yes, the wealth of this audience, had to have, one must say, a certain glamour to it. From the standpoint of the sensibility of the poor people of the barrio, it could not fully be their church. And from the standpoint of the visitor, it had to have a certain touristic character. Indeed, one could find the church in Rigüero by looking for the Turnica bus parked in front, having dutifully discharged its cargo, fresh, as very few travellers in Nicaragua can be, from their air-conditioned ride. For this reason, the existential quality of the experience, while real, is momentary. This is not to say that it could not lead elsewhere – as it is indeed meant to do, and as I suppose one could say it led in my instance. It is only to insist that there had to be limits to and divisions within the Church of the Poor, and in the relation to it established by an outsider from the metropolis. There was no avoiding this unless one took the way of a Theo and became completely immersed in the life of the common folk – even then bringing along as permanent baggage one's internalization of the ways of the metropolis. Short of that, one had to live with the differences, and try to be as conscious as possible. Certainly in my case, though I went one step further and lived in a community without glamour of any sort, without beautiful murals and without a charismatic preacher, I found that the 'necessities' of my life, which are usually not necessities but only sedimented choices, kept me from being as much a part of San Pablo as I might have hoped to be.

The people of San Pablo who stand out the most sharply in my memory were a venerable couple named Chepita and Octavio. They were both like gnomes: short, bright and gnarled. There is much dancing at the festivals of the community, and it seemed as if Octavio was always the first on the floor, moving in a stiff and stately way, with a wild shock of black hair and an emblemized T-shirt. 'I Sleep on Top: Summit Hotel', said one of these; but my favourite was the deep blue one with 'Hockey All Stars' blazoned across the chest in big white letters. What had been the journey of these shirts?

Chepita was slender, with taut skin and fine wrinkles. She could have been any age from forty to eighty, and looked as if she had lived all her life in the deep countryside, though in fact she had always resided in Managua. It is hard to believe, but as Marchetti said, when Chepita was a girl, much of Managua was countryside. Her legs were well bowed, testimony, no doubt, to rickets as a child; and it didn't look as if she could get very far on them. Yet earlier this year Chepita had gone with Foreign Minister Miguel D'Escoto and others (about eighty people, including Chepita and Pedro Joaquín, went the whole way, while certain legs of the journey had as many as two thousand marchers) on his *via crucis*, a walk of fifteen days and 326 kilometres from Jalapa, near the Honduran border, to Managua, to dramatize the call for peace – and of course to send a signal to Cardinal Obando, that there were Christians in Nicaragua who were ahead of him.

There is no established leader of the People's Church, but D'Escoto is clearly its bellwether, and has emerged at the opposite pole from Obando in the political schism of Nicaraguan Catholicism. I met Chepita again at a high-spirited celebration of D'Escoto's twenty-fifth year in the priesthood; and would see her from time to time in the streets of the barrio. Once she came to Pedro's with a stack of the weekly *El Tayacan* for distribution. I had not known she worked with that remarkable publication, which seemed as much a part of her as if it sprouted from her body.

EL TAYACAN

El Tayacan – the name is of a majestic tree native to Nicaragua – is the true voice of the People's Church, and a journalistic marvel. An enormous amount of printed material issues from the various institutions connected with the Church of the Poor, such as the journal *Envio*, Molina's Centro Valdivieso, the Jesuits and the University of Central America. It is mostly very good, but the reference point is the intellectual élite. *El Tayacan*, on the other hand, speaks to the people, and in their voice. In fact, there is no better way to acquaint oneself with Nicaraguan Spanish as it is spoken in the street than to read the weekly 'fotonovela' in *El Tayacan*. These are moral tales, told in comic-book form, and using photographs of actors in place of drawings (though the newspaper makes free use of the conventional comic-book form as well). The whole has an unprofessional look to it, which only heightens its subtle aesthetic quality. The fotonovelas are either the work of a skilled artist who knows how to efface him/herself, or of an indigenous artist of genius. The tales provide an excellent sense of the lived reality of the Nicaraguan people in this time of revolution and war.

Here is Doña Rosario reading the daily *Barricada*. The headline screams: 'Terrorismo criminal'; 'Maldito yanquis!' she exclaims, then receives a call that her only son may have fallen at the front. 'It cannot be', she says, then rereads his last letter and flashes back to her farewell scene with him. 'Her heart is a riverbed of sorrow, but she cannot cry.' She fears going mad with the suspense of not knowing his fate, turns to friends for solace, refuses their offerings of food and drink. 'I am alone, without husband, children or grandchildren. The only thing I want is to see my son once more, give him a kiss, then die.' Her friend, who is younger, remonstrates: 'the worst of your suffering is thinking you are alone. A pain between two is less of a pain.' 'But we all suffer alone', claims Doña Rosario. 'No one can suffer for another.' The young woman continues: 'Your pain is everybody's pain. Those who kill your son also want to kill your hope.' 'I don't know any more what hope is,' persists the despairing mother. 'I don't even know if God is more than a tale.' She goes to the front to seek her son. The officer in charge also tries to console her: 'You have to hope . . . what will be will be . . . hope that with your boy and all the others, we're going to triumph.' Still she despairs. 'It is the evil hour for Doña Rosario, the hour of the power of darkness', comments the text. She then hears from Doña Coco that her son is said to be alive, but still she refuses to believe . . . until she actually is reunited with the boy. 'Happy day, mamma!' The fotonovela concludes with a moral: 'Blessings to those who believe without seeing . . . that we will march towards life and victory.'

The blessing has an ironic bite: Doña Rosario cannot believe unless she sees, which is to say, she lacks faith. Her despair is a weakness, presented unsentimentally, yet she is also more realistic than her well-meaning neighbours. There is no easy comfort, no piously happy ending, because every reader knows of mothers whose sons have not returned. Such tough-mindedness is characteristic of the fotonovela. In another, 'Mario el descalzado' (a term for contras who return and receive amnesty), the first frame shows us the blood-smeared corpse of the peasant Pancho, murdered by contras. He was the older brother of Marina and Chepito, whose story is resumed a year later. Chepito tells Marina that her ex-boyfriend, Mario, who ran off to join the contra, has returned under the amnesty. He spends the rest of the novela futilely trying to convince Marina to forgive Mario.

The boy's innocent capacity to forgive – and his desire to make his sister happy and reinstate the older male in his life – are presented with great poignancy against the unforgiving reality. Chepito befriends Mario and acts as an intermediary between the old lovers; but Marina will not yield. 'Only you come to see me', says the ex-contra. 'There is still some fear of you among the people', the boy responds, and Mario agrees. 'But I don't fear you', says Chepito. 'Because you knew me from before.' 'Yes, and I want to become your in-law. But Marina won't forgive.' 'I know,' replies Mario, 'the contras are assassins and I have been no better than a dog. You forgive me because you come to talk with me, but she remains alone.' The boy keeps trying to bring them together, until Mario tells him to desist. 'The revolution has been generous to me, it gave me the opportunity to come back and work, but some things can never be undone. Even if Marina forgives me she can never be mine again. How many things have been lost in this war because of our guilt! I have lost Marina and I deserve this.' Here Mario is rendered sympathetically as a repentant, the boy Chepito is endearing, one senses that Marina has not allowed herself to come to terms with the situation, and Christian morality calls for mercy . . . and still there is no happy ending. For all its compassion, the tale refuses to resolve the dilemma. It is popular culture as tragedy.

A complex realism characterizes the *Tayacan* fotonovela at its best. Its simplicity should not be confused with simplemindedness, nor its cautionary character with lack of moral complexity. On the contrary, *El Tayacan* often achieves a degree of high seriousness I cannot recall seeing elsewhere in popular culture. Certainly it soars above the triviality, deceptiveness and frank irrationality we are accustomed to in our own media.

The journal also serves as the political voice of the People's Church. Most of the material here is predictable in its congruence with the views of the FSLN. At the same time, *El Tayacan* represents the specific interests of the radical Christian community in the national dialogue. Shortly before my arrival, an important issue appeared devoted entirely to the ongoing construction of a Constitution. For those who think democracy in Nicaragua is a farce, the development of a Constitution appears to be a trivial rubber-stamping of already chosen party policy. This is not a view held, however, by great numbers of Nicaraguans, who participate actively and directly in *cabildos*, or open town meetings in which the demands of one sector of the population or another are made known. Perhaps these Nicaraguans are deluded, but they act as if their voice makes a difference in the future of their country – and they are encouraged to do so by the government.

The issue of *El Tayacan* devoted to the Constitution consisted mostly of a number of animated presentations of the constitutional process as a guarantor of democracy, and of the virtues of participation and communality in the construction of a democratic society. This was presented as the will of God as revealed in the Book of Exodus:

> A Dios le gusta la democracia . . . en la Biblia leemos como Dios formó a su pueblo. Lo sacó de la esclavitud para que se fuera haciendo un pueblo de hombres libres y conscientes que participarán – en las decisiones colectivas – en la elaboración de leyes justas para el bien de la comunidad – en el proyecto común de construir una nación digna y soberana en medio de las demás naciones.*

Then two specific proposals are made for the constitutional assembly:

> That there be a bicameral legislature with a permanent *Cabildo abierto*, or open town meeting, counterposed to the National Assembly. The latter would embody representative democracy, and be composed of elected representatives chosen by the

* God likes democracy. We read in the Bible how God formed his people. He took them out of slavery so that they could make themselves into a free and conscious people who would participate – in collective decisions – in elaborating just laws for the welfare of the community – in the common project of building a dignified and sovereign nation among other nations.

political party; while the former would embody direct democracy, and consist of delegates of the various mass organizations – 'women, youth, workers, peasants, Christians . . . ' These organizations had played an important role in the provisional revolutionary government; but the general sense of political movement has been against them and toward a single chamber manifesting a more traditional form of party representation (though one in which minority parties could achieve a voice, in contrast to the United States Congress). The relations between the two houses of Congress are left unstated, though the impression is that the *cabildo abierto* would be a place where the immediate voice of the people could be heard, making demands upon, but not necessarily overruling the elected representatives.

That the name of God be left out of the Constitution, and that only some statement be made in the Preamble affirming that there was no contradiction between religion and revolution. The sense here is to move toward the separation of church and state, with formal guarantees of religious freedom – although it is not made clear here what sort of protection would be given to religious groups who oppose the revolution.

In its emphasis on community, local action, spontaneity and direct democracy, then, the Church of the Poor concentrates within itself all the anarchistic tendencies of the revolution, and opposes the statist or centralizing tradition. How this will fare is open to question. It would be naive to suppose that the liberation church commands a great deal of material power, or that it can be more than the conscience of the revolution. But this, of course, is no mean thing, especially for a government constantly struggling to achieve legitimacy. The 'spirit' of the Sandinist revolution comes forth here more than with any other group. And in a revolution, spirit is power.

CELEBRATION

The 'Celebración del XX aniversario del nacimiento de las comunidades eclesiásticas de base "Parroquia San Pablo Apóstol" ' stretched out over an entire weekend. Friday night was devoted to 'la comunidad comparte' – the community shares – and featured a bonfire and songs; Saturday was called 'la comunidad reflexiona' and was given over to talks reflecting upon the history of the community and the theology of liberation (this given by Uriel Molina), with music in the evening by Carlos Mejía Godoy and local performers; and Sunday morning – 'la comunidad celebra' – was to be a march from 14 Septiembre through the streets of the eastern barrios to the church at Ducuali, where a mass would be held.

The little church in 14 Septiembre was adorned with palm leaves and the images of its heroes and martyrs. A large sign, painted on a backdrop made from sewn-together hundredweight wheat bags, hung over the entrance and announced the event. Proud members sat outside issuing identity badges and registering names in a ledger book, while the children of the community, Joaquín Antonio Romero among them, scampered in and around the assembled visitors. There was dancing, led by Octavio in a red cap, along with hugging, laughing and chanting. The watchwords of the church, '¡Entre Cristianismo y revolución, no hay contradicción!', rang through the hall. And there was testimony. It seemed everyone had a voice, and while a good number of clergy were present, they were there to listen to the parishioners. Molina's talk was graceful and witty – in contrast to his sombre sermon – and proceeded despite the more or less obligatory breakdown in the amplifying equipment. He told of how in the past there had only been the Cathedral in Managua, high above the masses, whereas today the church was genuinely open to the people. Faith was now a matter of practice, not theory, and it had become inherently political, inseparable from political practice as such. All this had created a great crisis of identity in the established church, and we did not know how this crisis would be resolved. What Molina did not add – but everybody knew – was that the celebration remained ungraced by the presence of the Archbishop of Managua, although it had been a previous archbishop, twenty years before, whose permission had allowed San Pablo to be born. Obando y Bravo had been invited, but had not deigned to reply.

The procession had been scheduled for seven o'clock on Sunday morning. The sky was mushy when I awoke, and darkened rapidly thereafter. By 6.45 a deluge commenced and bid to continue indefinitely. Well, thought I, a little rain is not going to stop a bunch of revolutionary Christians. Why, they feed on suffering and hardship. So off I packed to San Pablo, rain gear in place and with visions of medieval sacrifice in mind. But there were only six people at the church, and they were in the process of cancelling the march as I arrived. Sensible souls. Now that the British empire is no more, the song about mad dogs and Englishmen being out in the midday sun should be amended to refer to gringos in the Managua rain.

The rain stopped, and the mass at Ducuali took place, attended by means of Pedro's Blazer. It was a gala affair by liberation church standards, with a number of the progressive priests in their regalia surrounding the altar, an abundance of music and a touching procession of women bearing images of the martyrs and a young soldier bearing a bunch of carrots. After it was over there was nothing further to do that day but watch the World Cup soccer matches (which Nicaraguans followed with great enthusiasm, rooting, as did the whole hemisphere, for the eventual victor, Argentina). The day was hanging, as Sundays will. I found myself, however, being more than usually tense as this one progressed. I wondered why; and then it occurred to me that the mass of the morning had left me restless, and that I had yet another mass to go to that evening, at the Casa de los Jesuitas.

Besides exceeding my lifetime average of religious occurrences per Sunday by almost exactly two, this affair was disquieting in its own right. For although Dr Mario Flores Ortíz was, as I have mentioned, the only individual in Nicaragua who intimidated me, the Jesuits had managed to intimidate me as a group. Perhaps it was their heroic tradition of rigour and discipline. Or perhaps it was the way they lived as a tight, closed circle of celibate and cerebral men. Holy as the Jesuits might be, they were also human beings, and such a social arrangement is not conducive to easy-going ways. My previous visits to the house in Altamira, usually made to leave a message for Peter Marchetti, had never been relaxing affairs. My first mass in such august company – and the second mass of the day – promised to be distinctly trying, as it would be conducted in very close quarters where my obvious unsuitability for this sort of thing would be made glaringly obvious. I could not bring myself to call the whole thing off, but I managed nevertheless to get thoroughly lost on streets that I knew rather well, and arrived at eight o'clock, the scheduled time for the mass, quite flustered.

The Jesuits were finishing dinner as I arrived. I had already eaten, which was just as well, because they were running out of food. Marchetti hobbled over, explaining that he had just returned from running his *repliegue*, in which he had distinguished himself by finishing ahead of a 76-year-old man who has been on every one of the races since the triumph of the revolution. I was offered toast and cacao, a local *fresco*, and accepted with alacrity, since I had got into the habit of eating whenever possible, and had a weakness, besides, for the drink. The cuisine in Nicaragua may leave much to be desired, but there is great pleasure to be had in the various punches, taken in the context of more or less continuous thirst.

It turned out that the eight o'clock time for the mass was to be understood in the Nicaraguan sense, as meaning sometime after nine. It also turned out that I had misjudged the emotional climate of the Casa de los Jesuitas. Obviously one's reception by a collective of intellectual priests is going to be different in tone from that given by peasants or workers. The spontaneity, the super-abundance of affection which a Chepita could express with her '¡hermano!' is out of reach for those who have been annealed in the furnace of The Word. But there is a fellowship which comes from sharing a common affection and common ideals. It is the friendship of the *internacionalistas*, raised here to the spiritual plane. This combination of faith and revolutionary commitment assures the visitor a loving welcome. The Nicaraguan generosity of spirit is here, too, even if it be a bit reserved.

The fact that the practitioners of the liberation church are open to revolution as well as faith accounts also, I think, for one of their most striking and endearing characteristics, namely, their good cheer. I have never met a more optimistic and cheerful group, even in the face of all the odds against Nicaragua, and its pain and torment, which they feel with the utmost keenness. There is nothing forced about their optimism, none of that 'positive thinking' which compulsively drives the Gospel of Wealth, nor can it be explained psychologically, on the basis of 'character types'. It is more akin, rather, to Pedro Joaquín's dignity, and comes from the same source

75

– a life put together so that it feels the growth inherent in every situation as well as, indeed as part of, the pain and suffering. This consciousness moves toward the poor and the oppressed, not for charity's sake, but because it senses the power and beauty contained there. It is like a tropism, a reaching for the sun.

It is easy to say that the Jesuits in Nicaragua are cheerful because they believe, and are convinced that God is on their side. This may be so but it explains nothing, at least in terms that a critical intelligence can accept. After all, Ronald Reagan is convinced that God is on his side, too, and I understand that he is quite a cheerful fellow. But there is a crucial difference between a belief which is grounded in a clear conscience and open to the suffering and hope of the wretched of the earth; and one which, on the other hand, dwells in the defence of the oppressors. The former opens the self and presses towards universality, lucidity and love; while the latter closes in on itself, becomes blind and clotted, and lives by delusion and paranoia. In practice it may be difficult to say which side of the line someone is on. The domain of 'spiritual politics' includes fascism as well as liberation, and the boundary between these can be very obscure in some instances. In the Casa de los Jesuitas in Managua, however, I felt that I knew where I was politically, with a clarity I cannot recall having attained elsewhere.

The mass took place out of doors, in the patio and bathed by the soft wind of a Nicaraguan night. Others had gathered, making the number of celebrants about fifteen. We were drawn into a circle. There were several elderly women, quite regal in bearing, and a talkative, funny old man whose name I forget. I was told later that he was the Comptroller of Nicaragua, one of the small but significant number of wealthy Nicaraguans who have thrown their lot in with the Sandinistas. There were young people too, some girls and a strikingly handsome, even beautiful youth who had recently been demobilized from his duties with the EPS, along with an intense young woman. Among the foreigners were George Gelber, an Englishman doing a human rights survey for the government of Sweden, and a Brazilian, whose name I also unhappily do not remember – a saintly man who works with Fernando Cardenal on popular education. To my sharp regret, Cardenal was not present. In fact, only four of the Jesuits were there: Marchetti, who bravely

76

fought off his fatigue for the duration of the mass, then retired; Xabier Gorostiaga, the political economist and director of the research institute, INEAS; Joe Mulligan, another Northamerican who works for the journal, *Envio*; and an elderly man named Luis, whom I took to be a Spaniard.

Gorostiaga led the service, if such a verb can be used. It would be more accurate to say that he set the pace and allowed for transitions to take place. There were essentially three phases: a period of scriptural reading, the Bible being passed around and people reading a paragraph or two aloud, each concluding with the phrase, 'la palabra de Dios' (the word of God); a period of testimony, rather like a Quaker service, individuals speaking as the spirit moved them, generally about religion and the revolution, or commenting upon some text; and the communion.

In contrast to the customary Catholic service, where the congregation lines up to receive communion from the priest – and by doing so, recapitulates the relation of authority and hierarchy – here the wine and wafer were passed successively around the circle, each participant taking her or his in turn. I am certain this is closer to the sense of the word used to denote the ceremony, and closer as well to the spirit of the original Christian gathering. What was uncertain was my relation to the process. I had been silent, principally out of shyness over my Spanish, in a situation where there was considerable choice and control over what happened. But now the body and blood of Christ were headed inexorably in my direction by virtue of my inclusion in the circle. There was no avoiding it. The thought flashed that my non-Christianity made it impossible to take communion, or at least that it was some kind of transgression – not that anybody would know or do anything about it. But thought cannot stay reality; and in the next moment the Eucharist was in my heathen hands, which engaged the wafer with the wine and placed it in my mouth. I passed on the substances to the person sitting on my left, and awaited the result: cataclysm, illumination or nullity. But of course (how can I use this phrase?) none of the above transpired. What happened instead was a sense (not a sensation) of being lifted up and spread out, a lightening, perhaps it can be said, of my Ego and a dispersal of my self – or to be more exact, a furthering of what was already taking place during the mass, and indeed, beforehand in the Casa de los Jesuitas and in Nicaragua as a whole. But these things are so hard to describe.

My greatest regret in Nicaragua was in not seeing the one person who would have surely disapproved of what had taken place that night – and of much else, besides, in my experience: Cardinal Obando y Bravo. The Cardinal was known to give a weekly mass in a little church on the outskirts of Managua. I wanted to go, to see how the other side worshipped, but a number of contingencies made it impossible for me to do so. I found out about the Cardinal's mass from the 'Conferencia Episcopal de Nicaragua', the head-quarters of the hierarchy. This is a sleek and discreet modern building behind an iron fence. It is only half a block from one of Managua's busiest streets, but it is on an unpaved road and seems far removed from anything. In fact, I passed it by at first, and stopped instead at another modern building, also well-protected but less sleek and more aggressive, which occupies the adjacent lot. This had some photos of an oriental gentleman and a brass plaque next to the door announcing that the edifice was the Embassy of North Korea. Wrong number. I returned to the incognito building, ascertained from a gardener that it was indeed the seat of Catholic power in Nicaragua, and knocked at the heavy wooden door. No answer; the place was closed. Returning in a few days, I managed to be admitted by a secretary, who fetched a stocky nun, very traditionally outfitted. She was extremely hospitable, plied me with *fresco*, told me of the Cardinal's schedule and that of the second-in-command, the even-more oppositional Bishop Vega (since deported), and asked me to return in a few days for a packet of materials explaining the church's stand.

This I did, and received a sheaf of papers bound together by a brown paper wrapper. The papers consisted of a theological précis explaining that the root of human problems was sin, whence we all needed to become reconciled to each other (in other words, the government of Nicaragua should allow the contras in); and a great many allegations of persecution of the church by the FSLN. Of these, there was only one for which I had any direct information, namely, the charge that on 3 March 1983, 'Sandinista mobs profane the Mass celebrated by the Pope in Nicaragua'. I know about this because I saw a film of the event, in which the 'mobs' included a group of mothers asking John Paul II to bless their seventeen dead sons, murdered only two days before by contra forces. The Holy Father paid no notice, and this had angered the huge crowd, which had come from all over the country to see the Pope, and which was essentially being scolded by him for not obeying the church hierarchy. The 'mob' then chanted '¡Queremos la paz!' (We want peace) and these inflammatory words visibly angered the Pontiff. Everybody parted on bad terms: an unhappy occasion indeed, but perhaps not described accurately by the Episcopal Conference of Nicaragua. I must leave it to others to determine if the other charges are of a similar degree of veracity. I know that something which looks a great deal like religion is more than tolerated in Nicaragua – and also that religion has been used to justify and sanctify, and even to commit, some of the worst crimes in the history of the human species.

On the very morning I had planned to attend Cardinal Obando's mass, Pedro Joaquín asked me if I was going to the services at San Pablo. He wanted me to go with him, and I could not say no. In any case, I wanted to attend. What I had seen so far of the Church of the Poor was either administrative or for public consumption. It was time to see their faith in its natural habitat.

As usual, things began late. The children were playing in front when we arrived, and they kept playing for the next forty-five minutes while everybody gathered. At a signal, they sobered down and filed in solemnly, taking their seats on one side of the church, which they occupied completely. I had expected a wholly indigenous service, but it was not to be. One of the priests who had officiated at the birthday celebration was paying a visit, and he was to give communion and a sermon. There was no wine for communion, and they had to make do with the local equivalent of a dry biscuit for wafers. I gained a further idea of the poverty of San Pablo when the collection plate was passed. The average donation was a ten or twenty córdoba note, the former worth a penny at the official rate of exchange and half that on the black market which is savaging the Nicaraguan economy. I gave 500 córdobas, which probably does not represent a fair expression of the economic difference between us, and would have given more were it not for fear of looking extravagant.

The priest also looked as if he felt out of place. He was a clean-shaven fellow with dark glasses and a worried expression. His sermon was full of tension and admonition. This was a special day (it is hard to find one that isn't in Catholicism, and that day would be special by its ordinariness), the festival of St Peter, founder of the church, and it led the priest to reflect on the institutional significance of the church. Human institutions, said the priest, needed guidance; in fact, they needed a single centralized authority, embodied in a leader. What would school be like, he asked the children, if there were no teacher? 'Everybody would go home', replied a child, to general laughter, but the priest was not to be distracted. And what would a factory be like if there was no director? 'It would be robbed,' said another child. No, said the priest, there would be no production. And that is why Peter's church needs a pope, to give it instruction and leadership. But the pope was not a 'superhombre'. He was only a man and could not do everything. Therefore the communities and local churches had to have responsibilities, too. The priest closed with a plea to parents. Encourage your sons to take up the vocation of the priesthood, he urged them. It is a good life – and besides, the church needs priests; there is a great shortage.

He might have added: and they could grow up to be pope. Or he could also have said that the reason the base communities arose in the first place was because of the lack of priests, which forced people to take their religion into their own hands if they were going to have it at all. I wondered if there had been any dissatisfaction with this sermon, which subtly but unmistakably undermined the base community. Later, Pedro confirmed that this was so. Such priests were a kind of fifth column, sent periodically by the hierarchy to co-opt and weaken the People's Church. The bishops cannot destroy the base communities, much as they may want to, because that is where Catholicism's dynamism resides. The Puebla conference of 1979 legitimatized the People's Church, and even the Pope has endorsed it. So they try to vitiate it and draw forth the next generation of priests from it. The people, meanwhile, are too

Homes near Puerto Cabezas

In the market, Managua

Selling yams in Puerto Cabezas

A meeting at an agrarian cooperative, Pueblo Nuevo

Pavel at home in his fortress

Clara with some of her children at the Cooperative Gamez–Garmendia; her husband Vicente is next to her; the elected leader of the cooperative is behind them

A soldier on the northern front, 1985

Commemorating
those fallen in the
struggle against the
dictatorship and
the counter-
revolution, in the
parish house, San
Pablo Apóstol

The church at San Pablo Apóstol, decorated for its twentieth birthday celebration

Near the dock, Puerto Cabezas

STEVE CAGAN

respectful to speak back. But if they could say what they felt, they would have answered, 'socialism!' to the priest's inquiry into what would happen if the factory director should be absent.

Once the priest sat down, the people did speak, in that style of spontaneous theology made famous by Ernesto Cardenal and the community of Solentiname. Pedro Joaquín was the first, and he reflected vigorously upon the symbolism in St Peter's name, which in the Spanish – 'Pedro' – links with the rock – 'piedra' – on which Peter's church was said to be founded. So the man and the church were one, and they were both part of the earth. The church reflected human action, or labour, but it was a labour of love, the expression of our love through our material activity. As the church is a rock and part of the earth, so is it of the people, who are part of the earth, and who transform it.

Yes, said another man. He had been one of the musicians, and I had been struck by the ardent expression in his eyes, which reminded me of a figure in a painting by Perugino. Yes, Peter himself was of the people. He was a worker, a fisherman, and a 'pobre' like us, a 'rudo' – rude, or rough man. Because of this the church belongs to the people. And we of San Pablo should pay tribute to Pedro Joaquín, the 'piedra' of this congregation, and our namesake of the saint. The people all shouted their assent to this and Pedro walked to the front while they sang to him. He beckoned to his son. The boy came and stood beside him for the duration of the eulogy; and Pedro stroked Joaquín Antonio's shining black hair.

4

LA
MUJER

MANY NICARAGUAN WOMEN live without men, even though Nicaragua is supposed to be a more traditional society where stable codes of conduct have been worked out between the sexes.

Before I moved in with Pedro Joaquín I stayed with Elsa Ruth Ugarte in a large modern house in a neighbourhood on the western end of Managua named Belmonte. Elsa Ruth is a steady, gentle woman, an ardent supporter of the revolution, and a teacher of mathematics at the National University. Elsa Ruth is single, but I always think of her as a widow. She lived for years with her younger sister, Mirna, a physician, Sandinista militant, and high-ranking official in the Ministry of Health. My stay with the Ugarte sisters had been arranged by the Ministry, in part because of the proximity of their house to the psychiatric hospital. Two weeks before my arrival, Mirna Ugarte, in a hurry to get from one meeting to another, perished in an automobile accident on the Carretera Norte, one of the numberless casualties of Nicaraguan roads, vehicles and drivers.

I heard the news in the United States, and for a while wondered whether my stay would be cancelled by bereavement. But Elsa Ruth was eager to have somebody in the house. She now lived alone, except for Benjy, a feisty little dog, and Daneela, a fourteen-year-old girl from the Atlantic coast. Daneela was one of eight children whose mother had recently died. Elsa Ruth had brought her to Managua, as an act of charity and to fill a void in her own life. The child – for Daneela looked and acted like a ten-year-old – went to school in the morning, where she attended the equivalent of third grade [primary school], hung around the house in the afternoon and indifferently swept the dust from here to there, and laboured over her homework with Elsa Ruth in the evening. She was painfully shy, and giggled and turned aside whenever I addressed her.

Though the house was spacious with tiled floors, and my accommodation was ample, there was a sepulchral feeling to life at Belmonte which made it easy to seek out the action of Casa Romero in the barrio 14 Septiembre. There was something, too, about the neighbourhood which made me shudder a little inside. I never had a sense of anyone else who lived nearby. It was rich but barren; and though Elsa Ruth was fortunate in one sense to live there, given the awful state of Nicaraguan housing, I think the loneliness of her own life was greatly aggravated by the absence of an immediate community.

Belmonte is one of those slices of bourgeois existence carved into the Nicaraguan countryside during the dictatorship. Sometimes these enclaves took hold, proliferated and became districts; and sometimes they just remained as small intrusions amid the over-whelmingly peasant character of Nicaraguan society. Belmonte was one of the latter instances. It was just a single street, really, of reasonably fine homes, with a few little offshoots. Surrounding it on all sides, and penetrating into the street at a number of points, was another world. A row of peasant huts ran parallel with the street on the south; while to the north was a shantytown of economically marginal and *lumpen* people. It was not at all unusual to see ox-carts rolling along the fine street of Belmonte, or pigs browsing about the lawns. This may sound cute, but there is nothing to romanticize about the ugly scars of poverty and class. For Elsa Ruth, this meant she had to live a double alienation – that of the neighbourhood itself, and that between the neighbourhood and its surroundings. One learned right away that, revolution or no, one's position on the street of Belmonte constituted a target for those who lived on the next block. I left a ten-cent plastic cup (which I used to fill the radiator of my car, the cap, irreplaceable in

Nicaragua, being lost and gone forever) outside for two minutes one day, and found it taken by the time I returned.

One week I was away from Managua. I returned to find Elsa Ruth and Daneela in a state of consternation. The house had been burgled one morning while they were out. My own room, which was locked, was untouched; but a great deal of jewellery and some appliances had been taken from the rest of the house. The burglars had entered by climbing a tree and dropping down onto the patio. Nobody in the neighbourhood had seen anything – because there was no neighbourhood, really, to look. Elsa Ruth's condition, shaken badly by the death of her sister, seemed to become further withdrawn with this insult to the integrity of her home. She now began to double lock all the doors, adding a huge orange cable lock to the front door, despite the fact that the burglars had not even bothered with the door. Of course this only heightened her sense of isolation. It was getting to look uncomfortably like the urban para-noia I had thought was a trademark of life in places like Manhattan.

But this was Nicaragua, and help was on the way. A few days later several nuns materialized. Sturdy and cheerful, they moved into the capacious dwelling and set about repainting it. Sisters had arrived, and were bringing community to Elsa Ruth's life. When I next visited, the extra locks were gone.

Nicaragua is held together by the society of women, as in the case of the family of Doña Julia Cuadra de Sacasa. We never knew her as Doña Julia, but only as 'the Abuela' (grandma), for she was grandmother to my daughter-in-law, and the centrepiece of the extended family arrangement in which my daughter-in-law lived. Thus the Cuadra de Sacasa family was the family I knew best in Nicaragua, and the one that was 'family' to me. Doña Julia is a widow of great faith and sweetness, and an advanced yet indeterminate age. She spends her days in a rocking-chair holding court in the sitting room of her house in Colonia Centroamérica. Sometimes a priest comes by, for Doña Julia and her daughters are deeply engaged in the People's Church and belong to the Base Community of Colonia Centroamérica. Often it's a neighbour, or a remote relative, or somebody come to use their phone. Always, the greeting is kind and warm: 'Pase adelante' – come in; you are welcome here.

Julia Cuadra brought ten children into the world, of whom nine survive. The tenth was a young man killed many years ago in, I believe, a motor accident. His picture hangs on the wall and is one of the few decorations in the house besides the iconography of Jesus Christ. I learned also that upon his death Doña Julia went into a deep depression, and was helped by the psychiatrist, Dr Mario Flores Ortíz.

Of the nine survivors, three are sons. All the males are against the revolution and all the females, including the *abuela*, support it to one degree or another. One son, a white-collar worker who happens to be married to a Salvadorean woman, has emigrated to El Salvador in order to be closer to the right-wing political climate in which he feels at home. I recall him as a passionate Sandinista-hater who interrupted his tirade against the communist perfidy into which his nation had been plunged to accompany himself on the guitar as he sang traditional Nicaraguan songs. Ironically, he lives today from hand to mouth in El Salvador, one step away from destitution because of the horrid economic situation. Meanwhile the ancient Renault he left behind became one of my principal, if most perilous and unreliable, means of transportation. His other anti-revolutionary brothers are both well-off and live in other parts of the city. I cannot recall ever having met them.

The house is not very big, and certainly not very fancy, but it is solid, and seems to have infinite elasticity. Two of the daughters live away, although one – the mother of my daughter-in-law – spends a considerable amount of time at the *abuela*'s house. This leaves four grown women living at home with their mother, along with a varying number of grandchildren, including a youngster severely traumatized by combat on the southern front against the contras. One of the daughters at home is married, with a husband away at the war; yet it seems to me that even when or if he is with her again they will remain at Doña Julia's, since it is there that the logic of her existence resides.

The television is almost always turned on at the *abuela*'s, though often nobody watches save the shell-shocked and chain-smoking grandson. Indeed, to an eye accustomed to Northamerican nuclear family ways, nothing much appears ever to happen at Doña Julia's. There seems to be no public life emanating from Casa Cuadra, no productive labour in the ordinary sense of the term, no sexuality, even no individuality. People – almost always women – wander in and out languidly, gossip and chatter away. There is always a greeting, always someone to help, sometimes a catechism group organized by Doña Julia. But nothing . . . well, nothing linear ever seems to happen. Things just go round and round. The masculinized, objectifying eye of the Northern industrial nations fails to see the individuality, the productivity, the creativity and the power emanating from this archetypally female nexus. Esperanza, Violetta, Argentina, Cha Cha, Leyla – they are there all the time, as women-in-the-revolution, as Nicaraguan women, as women under patriarchy, sheltered by the vastness of Doña Julia's faith and love. Their lives are woven together to form a firmament, now opening onto the historical transformation of the revolution.

And why has it been that in this family, support for the revolution distributes itself cleanly along gender lines, the men opposed, the women in favour? Perhaps a statistical fluke, but more likely the elementary truth that revolutions are for those who have not had, and against those who have. This, however, does not make things simple for women in the revolution . . .

SEXUAL OPPRESSION
La mujer exige la igualdad

Woman demands equality. The words ran across eight columns of *Barricada*, topped only by the superheading, 'Vibrante, caliente, libre, sin tapujos . . . Un Cabildo para la historia'. A full-page headline in *Barricada* is nothing to get excited about – in fact, I cannot recall seeing an issue with less than a full page headline. The rotting of meat in a government warehouse gets full-page attention, as does the latest Sandinista victory or contra atrocity in the field, an expression of support by Argentina, or Ronald Reagan's latest lie or threat. But there was something different about this one, something more *caliente* than the everyday high drama provided by Nicaragua's balancing act over the abyss.

'Vibrant, warm, free, with nothing hidden . . . a town meeting for history . . .' The article, by Gabriela Selser, began on the front page and occupied the entire back page of the issue of 11 June. It described in considerable detail a gathering of the night before, a *cabildo*, or open meeting of a thousand women from every part of the country and every social class. They had gathered to place their demands before the commission deliberating the substance of the new Constitution. Seventy-five women had spoken, and many others stayed on well past the four hours allotted. A number of my acquaintances excitedly brought up the subject the next day; and the ripple continued for days afterward. All agreed it had been the most dynamic of the *cabildos*. The sentiment was certainly shared by Selser, who concluded her article in phrases extreme even by Nicaraguan standards of journalistic · extravagance.

> Fue una noche histórica, memorable, electrificante, contundente y profundamente viva, nadie pudo evitar sentirse identificado. Anoche nació una nueva conciencia para todos. Después de este Cabildo ni hombres ni mujeres volverán a ser los mismos!

> It was an historic, memorable, electrifying, . . . profoundly alive night. No one could avoid feeling identified. Last night a new consciousness was born for everybody. After this town meeting, neither men nor women will ever be the same again!

This, it should be kept in mind, is from the official newspaper of the the FSLN. *Barricada* is the voice of the Sandinistas.

What had provoked such furore? What entitled sexual politics to move into the foreground of the revolution when the very survival of Sandinist Nicaragua seemed increasingly to be in doubt? Observers in the United States, when they concern themselves about Nicaragua at all, worry about whether the country is 'democratic' or not, whether religious freedoms are preserved, or freedom of speech, or political pluralism – in other words, about anything which would shed light upon the one question that obsesses the Northamerican élite: is Nicaragua becoming a bastion of Soviet communism on the 'American' continent? But the great majority of Nicaraguans are scarcely bothered about such things. They feel friendly towards the USSR, because it has helped them in a time of need, and they leave it at that. No one I knew in Nicaragua felt much of anything about a Soviet presence (I myself saw no Russians save a few doctors during four visits to

Nicaragua), and they would shrug or laugh if one preached to them about the danger of becoming a vassal of Moscow. Along with this, the average person has little concern about press freedoms or lack thereof. Nicaraguans worry greatly about the war and scarcity, to be sure, but mainly at the level of what to do about a threat to survival. In the sexual sphere, however, politics gets at the root of what it is to *be* women and men together, in a time when it might be possible to change this.

I kept finding myself appalled at the pain women and men felt towards each other in Nicaragua. I suppose a tendency to romanticize the revolution had kept me from seeing the reality behind the rhetoric and the impressive but limited changes of the first six years. It was hard to accept that these charming, loving and generous people could be living at such a crippled level of sexuality. But even had I been disposed to do so, the reality would have been elusive. Sexual oppression of the kind that marks Nicaraguan life gets adapted to, becomes ritualized, sanctified and rationalized by the law, and so built into lives that it goes without saying. A revolution that changes the distribution of political power does not change the distribution of sexual power – at first. It does change the consciousness of sexuality, though, and ignites the struggle for further change.

The women at the *cabildo* were insisting that they live in a society which for all its revolutionary appeal to equality, remains patriarchal in law and custom and matrilineal in fact. A single immense contradiction governs sexual politics in this country where the great majority of women raise families without a spouse or *compañero* yet suffer a legal system that protects the male and abandons the female, indeed, sees to it that women raise families alone. Instituted in 1904, the Civil Code of Nicaragua reflects the values of the Spanish conquest, and has barely been budged by seven years of revolutionary rhetoric. In 1982, more progressive legislation concerning domestic and family relations was passed, but the 1904 law was not abolished. This left judges, lawyers and the police free to continue applying the older, frankly patriarchal code – an opportunity many have freely taken. In the words of the Oficina Legal de la Mujer (Office of Woman's Legal Rights) the Civil Code 'imposes more prejudices than it gives privileges' to women.

One has to read these laws to believe them. Here is a sample of what is still (as of July 1986) on the books:

After divorce, wives are not to remarry for 300 days, while husbands are free to marry immediately. The logic behind this piece of juridical brilliance is that the wife may have conceived in the last days of the old marriage, which would 'create problems' for the new one.

A husband can divorce his wife if he discovers that she became pregnant before the marriage.

Illegitimate children can only acquire legal rights if the father recognizes them, nor can they inherit his property unless he specifically states that they can. A great many children are in this category, born to and raised by women who have been 'seduced and abandoned'. A case in point is Liliana, who took care of Romero's house. She had been impregnated by a married man, who then dropped her and refuses to recognize his son. In these cases, not only does the mother have all the burden of child care with practically no economic support, she actually loses legal rights over the child. This is the infamous *patria potestad*, an institution which, as one of the speakers at the *cabildo* put it, is 'verguenza de la humanidad entera', a shame upon the whole of humanity.

Rape is considered a 'private offence', and only becomes a crime if the victim complains. Even then, physical proof of penetration is required, and demonstrable lesions must be proven. Proof of blackmail, trickery, etc., on the part of the man will not qualify. Also, the previous behaviour of the victim is considered to see whether she has been a 'good girl' or not. A woman with an active sexual life can rarely prove rape in a Nicaraguan court.

There are no specific laws relating to the physical abuse of women. All such cases – and they are many – are covered under the criminal codes. In practice this means that the police minimize incidents of wife-beating, since compared to 'real crimes', they seem minor. It is also an easy matter for the man to shift the blame onto the woman in these circumstances.

Therapeutic abortions are only contemplated if the father or, in the case of unmarried women, parents request it, and three doctors assert the necessity. This is a debilitating condition in an intact marriage; for the typical Nicaraguan woman with no companion, it means that any abortion will have to be illegal. It may also be recalled that much of the Nicaraguan population scarcely has access to one doctor, let alone three.

A woman who has an illegal abortion, i.e., the typical case, is liable for jail sentences of one to four years.

What is law and what is practised are, of course, two different things. As far as I know, for example, no Nicaraguan women are serving time in jail for having illegal abortions. In fact, the chief of the Sandinista police, Doris Tijerino, has publicly repudiated the law and has stated that the police will make no arrests of women in such cases. From another angle, though the legal structure may not have changed very much, most people agree that many social conditions for women have improved since the triumph of the revolution. I have heard of instances where a man harassing a woman on the street was set upon quite severely by passersby, and speedily arrested by the police. And the revolution has enacted legislation which has materially benefited women. Perhaps the most significant, and certainly the most strikingly visible, is a ban on any advertisement that represents women or the female body for the purpose of selling a commodity. (Imagine what such a law would do to our own cultural landscape.)

This is all to the good, but it does not mitigate the oppressiveness of the domestic codes. Patriarchal laws create a climate of hardship and injustice for women, and aggravate every difficulty they may suffer as a result of economic disadvantage or social prejudice. I was told that the Nicaraguan legal code is fairly representative of Latin American countries. However, the Nicaraguan revolution is anything but representative; and it crashes head-on into this sclerotic structure. Something close to open sexual warfare is the result.

Consider what was learned by María de Zúñiga. A Minnesotan by birth, María is the founder and director of an organization called CISAS, which helps Nicaraguans achieve self-reliance in health care, by, among other means, workshops on personal issues. When the subject turned to women's sexuality earlier this year, the

91

results turned explosive. There were five workshops involving a total of 133 women. Four of the groups consisted of members of the farm-workers' union in different regions of the country; and the fifth was of women visiting a health centre in Villa Venezuela, one of the poorer barrios of Managua. The women were of all ages up to sixty, though the majority were younger than thirty; and they had a total of 325 children and 31 *compañeros* between them.

The women were asked a number of questions, among them, to give their first association to the words, 'mujer' and 'hombre'. This is raw data, and no one would claim that the results of the survey amount to scientific proof. About a third of the women didn't respond, while the others were undoubtedly influenced by the group setting and had, of course, many other feelings as well. Taking all this into account, it is impossible to avoid the conclusion that males are fairly loathed. Fifty-seven of seventy-two responses were frankly hostile to men, and included choice epithets such as the following:

> slothful, womanizing, drunkards, irresponsible, traitorous, humiliators, ingrates, opportunistic, abandoners, dishonest, imbeciles, egoistic, shameless, evil, executioners, despised, jokers, offensive, lying, farcical, prideful, loafers, bossy, cowards, wolves, brutes, coarse, vicious, vain, capricious, woman-beaters.

And of course, repeated again and again, 'machistic'. Meanwhile the positive images range from tepid and nearly-neutral, for example 'worker', or 'useful', to the ambiguous 'some are good fathers', and but two unambivalent associations: 'brave' and 'beloved'.

The views of their own gender are a mirror of this. Of the forty-three positive images women have of themselves, most are of moral qualities having to do with being responsible or caring; while some have to do with bravery, strength and intelligence. Only one is frankly aggressive, one woman associating (I can imagine, to much laughter): 'will kill the man'. The thirty-three negative responses, on the other hand, are almost all of victimization. Women are

> marginal, discriminated against, martyred, tricked, un-appreciated, wretched, lack prestige, humiliated, exploited,

desperate, bitter, miserable, abandoned, needing fathers [for their children], tormented, disconsolate, suffering, abnegated, slaves, objects of commercialization, and sheep.

This is sexuality in the classical Latin American machistic mould, itself a variation on the themes of master and slave, or sadist and masochist. And the mould is cracking. One party, the male, cruelly abuses the other, the female, abandoning and humiliating her, and treating her as an object, an animal and a means only to his fleeting gratification. But the women fight back, inspired by the revolution; indeed, the very candour of the responses to María de Zúñiga's survey is a sign of an activated consciousness – a sign that women are not going to stand their abuse any more.

It might be thought that after six and a half years of social revolution, relations between the sexes would be more tranquil. But that is not the way a revolution works. Where there has been oppression, there is suppressed rage. Revolution is going to bring this to the surface, perhaps only in bits at first – remember the response, 'will kill the man' – but enough to trigger counter-violence. And the fact has been that the counter-violence of the once dominant is generally more severe and punitive than the violence of the oppressed. This is true in the sense that counter-revolutions are usually more violent than revolutions; and it is true in the sense that macho violence toward women grows as women begin to assert themselves. Nicaraguan men are much less likely than progressives from the United States to be happy about the strides made by Nicaraguan women since the triumph of the revolution. Many men may have embraced the feminist cause, but many others – and of all political stripes from Left to Right – have been opposed and feel deeply threatened. The whole macho complex is built on weakness in the first place – on a fear of the female and a dread of intimacy and passivity – and it only gets aggravated when the victim refuses to play her submissive role any longer. Wilma Castillo, who is in charge of psychological services for the Oficina Legal de la Mujer, said in an interview that many, perhaps the majority of cases of wife-beating brought to her attention are incited by strides toward independence by the woman – say, by going out to get a job. When we consider that the stresses of life have greatly increased alcohol consumption, and add the numberless hardships of the economic crisis and, above all else, the war, with its movement of women into traditional male jobs and ceaseless displacement of people, the wonder is that any stable relations between the sexes survive.

The Oficina Legal was founded in 1983 as a unit of AMNLAE (Asociación de Mujeres de Nicaragua – Luisa Amanda Espinosa), the women's organization of Nicaragua, and has since become AMNLAE's most forceful component. Its premises exude a purposeful activity; indeed, it was the most efficient-looking and energetic Nicaraguan bureaucracy of my acquaintance. There usually seems to be some foreign delegation present, while troubled but hopeful-looking women congregate about the desks, seeking a lawyer, social-worker or psychologist to tend to their grievances. By giving women hope, OLM stirs the pot of sexual turmoil in Nicaragua. But it also works toward reconciliation, counselling men and helping couples to work through their difficulties.

There was another side to María de Zúñiga's study. The women were strikingly ignorant about sexuality. In another workshop involving two hundred women of all classes and levels of education, only ten knew that they were most fertile on the fifteenth day of their menstrual cycle. There is a widespread belief among the campesinas that talking of menstruation will make it stop, which may account for some of the ignorance. This, however, does not explain the fact that well-educated women are often just as much in the dark about the most elementary workings of their bodies.

The findings are part of a pattern; however swiftly it may be moving and despite all the stereotypes about 'hot' Latin countries, Nicaragua is sexually a very repressed place. According to one gynaecologist, fully 96 percent of her patients never experience orgasm. The body itself is repressed. Women by and large refuse to use tampons for their menstruation, because to do so would mean touching their genitals. For the same reason, the diaphragm is out of favour as a means of contraception, thereby putting a serious crimp in Nicaraguan efforts at birth control (something most women endorse, despite their Catholicism). With the diaphragm ruled out by reason of prudery, intrauterine devices are probably the most desired means, despite their many serious dangers and drawbacks. IUDs, however, are only sparsely available to the Ministry of Health – perhaps, as charged earlier this year by Oscar Flores, head of Women's Services, because bureaucrats hostile to birth control are withholding them. Private doctors can install the IUD, but for a fee of 25,000 córdobas, an average month's salary.

Condoms also require too much manipulation, though this is less of a problem than with the diaphragm. On the other hand, more of them are needed, which means confronting Nicaragua's poverty and exclusion from the world market. I heard of shipments of condoms arriving from Eastern bloc countries so dried out that they cracked upon removing them from their wrapping. Finally, use of the pill also suffers from short supply and the vagaries of a population as sexually ill-informed and repressed as Nicaragua's. Even so, many women seek out anti-contraceptive pills at places like the Huembes market. Here bins are filled with every kind of pill, freely available without prescription. People shop for them as though they were onions. It is a pathetic testimony to the dumping of drugs on the Third World market, and the magical value ascribed to Western technology.

In sum, Nicaraguans who are poor and want to limit their families have to make do with the rhythm method, the favoured means of the Catholic church. A professor of mine at medical school once told the class that there was a word for couples who used the rhythm method of birth control. The word was 'parents' – and indeed, there is no end of parents in Nicaragua, most of them single women.

The institution of marriage does not thrive in Nicaragua. I'm not sure why, but the fact seems to be that Nicaraguans avoid being legally married, even though there are practical advantages attached. A major issue in the current constitutional debate on sexuality is whether to give the *uniones de hecho*, or common-law marriages, the same legal protection as lawful marriage. Perhaps the eschewal of matrimony has to do with a healthy distrust by women of being ensnared, and the perception of how biased the system is. Or it may be a function of social class, weddings, whether in or out of the church, being distinctly more of an urban and middle-class phenomenon than a rural or lower-class one. As far as

I know accurate statistics do not exist, but the impression of informed observers is that the peasantry hardly marries at all. According to Peter Marchetti, who has worked for years with *campesinos*, only three percent of people who live deep in the countryside wed. This gives rise to some complications among a people who are profound believers even if they have little use for the institutional trappings of the church. A custom of the peasants offers a kind of resolution: the couple agrees to 'separate' a few moments before the death of one of them. Through this device, which beautifully combines piety and shrewdness, neither will be damned for dying in a state of sin, while their conjugal love will be preserved until the last thirty seconds of life.

The vignette reminds that there are intact and affectionate Nicaraguan couples who manage to avoid being shattered on the reefs of patriarchy and revolution. I became acquainted with two of this unusual breed during my stay, each very much part of the revolution.

I have already written something of the Romeros, Pedro Joaquín and Ligia, mainly from the perspective of the husband, the 'rock' of the People's Church. Pedro did seem to occupy the bulk of the space in that home. He had the project, and the mission; while Ligia had a job and a role. They were loyal to each other, but went their ways. In the weeks I stayed with them, I do not recall seeing the Romeros doing anything public as a couple. For them, there was a private world they shared, and a public world, which was the husband's. There were many women activists in the People's Church, but Ligia was not one of them. I do not even know if she was a *creyente*, though I know she went at times to church functions; just as I cannot really place her as a Sandinista, though I know she supported the revolution. Ligia worked outside the home and left the domestic chores to Liliana (even when Liliana went back to visit Estelí for a few days, Ligia did no cleaning, but brought in an older woman from the neighbourhood for the purpose). This, however, only introduced some middle-class features into the Romero household without dissolving the barrier between the sexes. Their relations remained quite traditional even if there was no feeling of patriarchal authority. When company came over, the women went deeper into the house and did their talking together about personal and domestic affairs, while the men stayed in the front sitting-room and discussed political and public matters. Inside and outside: the way it seems to have always been. It reminded me of gatherings at my parents' home during the fifties.

In writing of Ligia I feel baffled – more, sucked into the vortex I have known so many times: the (white male) expert pontificating about a woman's soul. Shades of old Freud wondering what women really want. But that was the way it was set up between us. My coming there was for Pedro's project; but I came bearing the stigma of a professionalism which was probably the thing about me she understood best. Such was the prism through which our relations were diffracted.

I think that Ligia would say she was happy with her lot. Yet she seemed to me to be full of longing and unfinished business. The integration that marked her husband's character had passed Ligia by, leaving behind desire. She would sing sentimental and revolutionary songs in a reedy voice. I had heard the songs before, from other throats, and they were full of optimism and ardour. But when Ligia sang them they made me sad. Her family had scattered, mostly to California, and I think she missed them greatly. She missed something greatly. Could it have been another child? She said that Bayardo Arce, Liliana's infant, would grow up not knowing which of the two women in the house was his real mother, so much did Ligia bounce him up and down, cuddle and sing to him. She seemed at times to be babysitting for Liliana while the latter hewed and fetched at the endless tasks of the household. Thus baby Bayardo, named by an admiring Liliana after the Comandante with the worst reputation in the US press for hard-line Marxist-Leninist tendencies, was getting a traditional Nicaraguan infancy, with a mother seduced and abandoned, and raised surrounded by women who showered him with endless love while abnegating themselves. Is this the matrix of a national character, generous and spontaneous, without fear or need of authority – a people defined by father-absence and identified with the mother? People like this may lack the work-discipline of the Teutonic North, but they are freer to make a revolution and give of themselves as they had once been given to. Yet how can a true revolution leave women in their position of abnegation?

If baby Bayardo Arce was close to the Nicaraguan norm, young Joaquín Antonio, as the only child in a nuclear family, was not. But he too was an extraordinarily affectionate youngster, and treated with equivalent affection by both parents. Skinny as a stick figure, he had a way of appearing suddenly in my room or by my side. He would announce himself by an abrupt 'Joel!' and wait to see what happened next. Sometimes we would share what I was doing. In this manner I taught Joaquín something of the ways of the little electronic typewriter on which I prepared my journal, a device which had duly impressed the whole family with its marvellous Japanese technology. Sometimes we simply tussled; and sometimes I read with him the Cuban books which comprised his very modest collection. One was a dictionary–atlas of Latin America; and another a lovely little work about chess, a game for which, to my disappointment, he evinced no interest.

Joaquín Antonio, though obviously bright, was an indifferent student, and this was the source of some grief and pain in the Romero household. Pedro seemed not to mind; but Ligia the schoolteacher took her frustration out on the boy for his laxness, scolding regularly and, sad to say, spasmodically striking him on a number of occasions. They were developing a scenario to grace a family therapy text – the mother pushing, the boy passively resisting. It rang true to nuclear family and middle-class ways in Northamerica, where the child is often placed onto the wheel of performance by a mother trying to live an unlived life through him, and punished for a failure he feels designated to repeat. My presence as the outside expert rounded out the pattern. I was duly consulted on how to instil some industry into the youngster, a task I discharged in the least intrusive way I could, mainly by reassuring Ligia that Joaquín was basically all right and that he would straighten himself out best if he were rewarded for good work rather than punished for bad. It was painful to watch this puppy-like boy get his dose of the Reality Principle, gratifying to be able to do a tiny bit to mitigate the tension.

The other family inhabited the same revolution but a different world, far from the city and without a trace of the middle class. I only had a few hours in their presence, but they are not hours I am going to forget.

The Cooperative Gamez–Garmendia occupies some 2,800 acres of steeply rolling, dramatic land high in the hills surrounding Estelí. Gamez–Garmendia (the hyphenation signifies the union of two units into one) represents the bedrock of the Nicaraguan revolution: an independent and liberated peasantry loyal to the Sandinistas. It is these cooperatives that the contra work hardest at destroying, and with good reason, for if the cooperatives succeed in this basically agrarian society, the revolution will be inviolable.

I spent the morning of the Fourth of July 1986 at this spectacular cattle ranch, while my countrymen were celebrating the unveiling of the refurbished Statue of Liberty. Elsewhere in rural Nicaragua that day, the people of San José de la Bocay were gathering the bits of thirty-three corpses which had been scattered by a contra landmine over which a truckful of peasants had passed the day before. I did not learn of the atrocity until later, since Gamez– Garmendia – over whose roads I too had passed in a truck the day before – has no facilities for getting the news. In fact, it has no electricity at all, nor plumbing. But it is fairly well protected, by a Sandinista army detachment whose signal tower can be seen between the trees on the other side of a nearby hill, and by its own thirty-one men, four of whom stand armed guard each night.

It is probably just as well I did not know of the attack on San José de la Bocay as I lay on the stone floor of the main house and wondered whether the sound of pigs snuffling about was a detachment of Ronald Reagan's Freedom Fighters, M16s in hand, come to get us. I suppose one gets used to this, but not the first night. After all, despite the relatively protected location (in contrast to pueblos like San José, which are pretty near indefensible, a Spanish nurse having been killed there in another mine blast six weeks before), my hosts were able to point out places within view where battles had taken place a year ago. The aura of menace is doubly bizarre inasmuch as the cooperative itself exudes a calm and organic security. I think this came from the spirit of the people, all of whom had been objects for others and were now the subject of their own lives. When a little girl can go freely to the corral and help herself to the milk freshly drawn from the cow – and from any cow, by any milker – and not have to worry what the *patrón* will do, because she and her people are the *patrones*, then a trusting spirit is

99

present. The sense of peace comes from the absence of domination, which is why, I suppose, the Big *Patrón* sends his mercenaries.

I had come with Rita, of the clinic, and Edwige, a journalist friend who wanted to do a story on the cooperative for her magazine, *Pensamiento Proprio*. Rita knew the place well. She had worked there in 1985 with a brigade of Northamericans who built eight houses, and was much beloved by the *cooperantes*. We had to park our car several kilometres from the centre of the cooperative because of the unforgiving road. It was then we met some of the men coming back from town on their new Toyota four-wheel-drive truck, the gift of a foreign government – if I recall correctly, Denmark. This truck, by the way, was literally the only piece of mechanized technology on the cooperative, and practically the only manufactured one; they used a plough, for example, which was the replica of one I had seen in a book on the Mayan Indians.

After the usual '¿Qué tal?'s and 'Más o menos's had been exchanged, we were escorted to the main building. This had been the home of the *patrón*, who was now living comfortably in his Estelí townhouse on the money with which the government had purchased his land. It was anything but luxurious – indeed, I thought at first it was the barn – but it was solid and spacious, and had some communal rooms, in contrast to the miniscule homes built by the *brigadistas*.

Here we met Doña Clara, wife of Vicente, who had been one of the men on the truck. I feel odd about giving Clara a title, since she was, after all, a *campesina* through and through, and had no formal standing in the community (which was governed by officers – males, of course – elected yearly). Certainly her husband, who was a stringy, exceedingly laconic peasant with a stubble of beard and several missing front teeth, would not have been called 'Don Vicente'. But I want a word to set Clara apart, to signify the impression she made, which was of regality.

Clara had the same dignity I had found in Pedro Joaquín, the same ripeness of soul. I know much, much less about her, to be sure, indeed, we barely exchanged ten words in the eighteen hours I spent at the cooperative. But there are certain things one learns about people from their bearing and their situation, and for Clara, Doña Clara, these things were transparent. She had borne nineteen children in her forty-five years or so of life. Fifteen of the children were alive and thirteen were living at the cooperative, including a son who had recently been demobilized from the army and had joined the cooperative with his own wife and infant. We expect a woman who has brought so much life into the world, feeding and tending to her children, fretting when they became ill and grieving when they die, to be worn down by ceaseless and unremitting toil. But Clara seemed to have filled out. With the exception of heavy varicose veins, her body showed no sign of its multitudinous labours. There was rather a kind of perfection in her physique, a radiation of power. The dignity of her spirit was incorporated into her broad shoulders and white teeth, and the fine, weathered impassivity and clear gaze of her Indian features.

Clara had been a cook in the *patrón's* household before the revolution, and Vicente, a farmhand. Thus they were the senior members of the cooperative, the fact which, along with their immense brood, earned them the farmhouse. Here she continued to cook her beans, process her exquisite cheese, grind her corn on a hand-mill and make her tortillas on a *metate*, from before the sun came up until the oil lamps flickered low at night and the last whimpering child was put to rest. I do not think any three people I have known have together done the work of this smiling woman, or created so much.

I asked if I could help in the morning and was shown the hand-mill. By grinding the corn for my tortilla that day I made the only direct, muscular contribution to my sustenance during my stay in Nicaragua. The rest was money and words. I do not intend to slight these means, any more than I intend to become a *campesino*. But it is necessary, I think, to recognize without breast-beating and crocodile tears just how parasitical the upper classes of humanity, and of course the 'upper nations', are on the labour of the majority – and how much we owe them. It is remarkable how such an experience, slight and indeed trivial in comparison to the labours of a Clara or a Vicente it may have been, writes a message on the body that sharpens one's appreciation of what it takes to keep life going. I can feel the pain in my shoulder, the need to switch to a two-handed stroke, as I write this. (For the record, Clara ground corn with one arm.) The corn out of which tortillas are made is not the tender vegetable we enjoy directly from the cob, but tough and leathery, and makes you work to put it in condition for eating. The heavy physical labour done sixteen hours a day by a Clara is never rewarded or valued like the labour of the head; but if there were some kind of just calculus that compensated people proportionately to the effort they expend, the Claras of this earth would be the wealthy ones.

It cannot be put in the scales of compensation, but the dignity that comes from giving one's self completely to life and bringing so much forth is a kind of reward. Who could have more integrity? More, a Clara, though she be poor by all monetary measures, is wealthy in her community and in Nicaragua because she has the esteem of all about her. The revolution has not made Clara and Vicente rich – though there is much wealth in that land – but it has honoured them by giving them control over their life. Compare the fate of comparable people in El Salvador and Guatemala, or Brazil, or the Philippines, and you will have no difficulty in appreciating the logic of the Central American revolution.

But there is a deeper, more ambiguous side to all this. Nicaragua gives Clara more than honour, and in so doing takes away from her too. People like Clara are more than honoured. They are venerated and inserted into a myth. Because Clara is not just a woman, or a cook, or a *campesina*, or even a mother. She is *Mother*, an archetype, a myth, perhaps the most important myth in Nicaragua, or at least the most tenacious and rooted, and the one which most entwines itself about women. We might say that Doña Clara is the Doña Julia – the *abuela* – of the countryside, a Doña Julia with hands upon the production of the means of life, hence a figure of mythic proportion.

There is nothing unique about Nicaragua here; I doubt there exists a traditional society without a nuclear myth of the all-powerful, all-giving mother. Any society which relates directly to the earth, which is to say, any pre-capitalist society, fuses maternal power with nature itself. Nations bring these myths with them as they enter modern history, and twist them about as their history dictates. For us, the female archetype became vitiated as modern society conquered and deadened nature; later she returned as 'Mum', a protecting figure to sacrifice herself and shelter her men and children from the harsh world. For Nicaragua, who was conquered, raped repeatedly and made into the provider for a satrapy of dictators, freebooters and Yankee warlords, the identity of the nation, its strength and hope for the future lay in the preservation of the power of the Mother myth. People like Clara, who succeed in living that myth, draw power from it. I think the charisma of the woman cannot be understood otherwise.

The Nicaraguan Mother is a vastly more powerful figure than our Mum, and she is actively worshipped. Mother's day in Nicaragua is a much greater affair than it is in the US. Many businesses close, and the press covers the event as if it were the World Series. This year, the paper *Nuevo Diario* ran an amazing photo, which I was told had been repeated from the year before, of a radiantly happy young mother, bare-breasted and with twins suckling on each teat. The image of Mother pervades Nicaraguan culture. Recruiting advertisements for the Sandinista army on television, for example, differ greatly from similar fare put out by the US military. Where US commercials have as their slogan, 'Be all you can be', show a father sending a boy to war when they show any parent at all, and emphasize how much technical skill the recruit is going to acquire, the Nicaraguan version will focus on the solidarity of the soldier with his people, and especially his mother. In one such commercial the denouement is a scene in which the young soldier is hugging his mother, the scene fading out on the image of the mother's face.

In the same vein, I chanced to see the Nicaraguan version of the official US army newspaper, *Stars and Stripes*. It is called *Segovia* (named for the region of General Sandino's campaigns, which is also where the cooperative Gamez–Garmendia is located), and it unashamedly plays upon the soldier's love for his mother. This is because the mother in Nicaragua, in contrast to her Northern counterpart, is an active source of power throughout the life cycle. The cover shows a great big youth in military dress being hugged by his mother, powerful-looking though a head shorter. Underneath runs the caption: 'Madre tu fuerza es nuestra fuerza / juntos forjaremos la VICTORIA' (Mother, your force is our force / together we will forge victory). The centrefold consists of a photo-montage of images of mothers and soldiers, and poems to mothers, and has the slogan, 'Las madres de los Héroes y Mártires son la Conciencia de la Patria' (Mothers of heroes and martyrs are the conscience of the nation). Yet another article consists of excerpts of letters sent by young soldiers ('Los cachorros' – cubs) to their mothers.

In view of this, a super-mother like Clara is closer to being a goddess than a curiosity. Her dignity is as profound as the myth it realizes. But there is a catch, which may be revealed by a comparison with Pedro Joaquín Romero. In putting his life together as a Christian–Marxist–Sandinista, Pedro Joaquín makes himself an historical agent. He lives in time. By living her life as the Primal Mother, Clara steps out of time. He lives in history – the given male role; she lives in nature – the given female role: powerful, noble, but locked in place. And the nature she lives in is also constructed by men: it is a 'second nature', inserted into the culture of a male-controlled power structure. The political and economic power of the cooperatives resides with the men, and all the land is owned through them. The female goddess who is worshipped in a male-dominated society becomes an object for that society.

Most of us would not want to share this fate. We live in time and value the self-transformation from which the Mother is excluded. The archetypal mother sets life into motion but is herself unmoved. More to the point, Nicaragua lives in time, and the lives of its women are swept along with history. Their genuine dignity depends on the degree to which they can make their history actively rather than being passively inserted into its mythic apparatus. The challenge is not to abandon tradition but consciously to recreate it within an unfolding historical dynamic. Practically speaking, this requires controlling some portion of what the community produces. Here Clara is fortunate. The women of Gamez–Garmendia have begun to develop their own industries within the cooperative. Their special project is a fishery, to be established in a pond near the main house (the cooperative is fortunate, too, in having plentiful water from springs). This enterprise will be exclusively the women's. It is being carried on with the permission of the men, whose monopoly over production it breaks. Similar ventures have been undertaken at other cooperatives; indeed some cooperatives are completely given to women (and administered with the help of

CEPA, the Centro de Educación Popular Agrario, a rural development association linked with the liberation church). These women,
Clara among them, have a genuine opportunity within the
revolution to enter history without losing their rootedness.

Most Nicaraguan women, however, are distinctly less fortunate.
For them the only pathway which lies open is that of a motherhood
subject to all the violent disadvantages of the Nicaraguan female.
Many women, I have been told, have given up on conjugal life
altogether. They find a man, induce him to impregnate them and
then go their own way without any effort at living with the father.
At least this gives them a child to love and some respect in
Nicaraguan society. And it also binds them closer to their own
mother. Thus they actively anticipate the abandonment which they
have every reason to expect will happen to them in any case. They
have retained the personal side of motherhood without the
grounding in a productive setting, and without security. It is an
understandable, but a hopeless, position. Pavel's mother, without
hope of work, wandering through the neighbourhood, hallucinat-
ing, and taking apart her house while neglecting her children, is the
extreme but logical implication of this type of existence. She is
mad, indeed is the Nicaraguan Mad Housewife, and excites the
horror and pity of the community – and she is also a tragic figure
epitomizing the nightmarish predicament of Nicaraguan women.
Tragic and, oddly enough, heroic too. As with most instances of
madness, there is resistance and protest in Pavel's mother. Like
Melville's Bartleby the Scrivener saying 'I would prefer not to', her
destructiveness is also a refusal to play the game of abnegating, all-
giving mother: it is a reminder to the society that it, too, should not
tolerate such things.

In the United States, women also suffer major economic
disadvantages, and great numbers raise children without fathers,
increasingly by choice. Other points of similarity could also be
drawn. After all, neither society has an exclusive patent on
patriarchy, and both have known the struggles of feminism. Indeed,
the Nicaraguan revolution, in contrast, say, to the Cuban, belongs
to the same historical phase that saw the coming of age of a global
women's movement in the 1970s. It drew energy from feminism;
and from the start has shared an identity with the international

women's movement. As in the United States, progressive people have widened the scope of their efforts from the overcoming of inequalities and injustices to the full emancipation of women, including that of sexuality. Sexual politics in the two countries have a lot in common then. It would be a major mistake, however, to disregard the deep differences between the two situations.

First, it is scarcely necessary to point out that Nicaragua and the United States stand at the extremes of the political spectrum. Nicaragua, for all its backwardness, is a highly revolutionary society where rapid social change is both possible and widely sought; and the United States, for all its advanced features, is a society whose business it is to crush revolution wherever it appears. The US is more than non-revolutionary: it is anti-revolutionary. In Nicaragua the centres of power are on the side of revolutionary forces, while in the United States the centres of power are almost exclusively preoccupied with defending the *ancien régime* and rolling back any revolutionary challenge to it. On a political level, therefore, Nicaraguan women can count on a high degree of support from the Sandinistas – for example, in the coverage by *Barricada* of the women's *cabildo* – while the most women in the United States can expect from the power structure is the bitter tokenism of appointing Sandra Day O'Connor to the Supreme Court and Jeane Kirkpatrick as Ambassador to the United Nations, or the slap on the back from mass culture: 'You've come a long way, baby.'

However, things are more complicated than this simple polarization would suggest. This is because the 'backward' features of Nicaragua and the 'advanced' features of the United States have very major implications for the sexes. The difference goes deeper than the fact that there has been a tradition of women's agitation for more than a century, as well as a widely influential (though certainly not universally accepted) movement for sexual enlightenment in the industrialized nations, and little to speak of in Nicaragua, or in the whole Third World, for that matter. Sexual codes and practices are not conjured up arbitrarily. They emerge out of the real conditions of life – conditions separated by an enormous tract of historical development from the First to the Third World. To ignore this, and to import the sexual standards of the industrial nations as though they were Toyotas is a serious mistake. A Toyota can be made to work on a Nicaraguan road. All it needs is a four-wheel drive and a heavy-duty suspension (a Diesel engine doesn't hurt, either, the fuel being unrationed). But Northamerican sexual mores and Nicaraguan social conditions are not at all compatible.

The recognition that women have equal sexual capacities and rights has been made possible by an erosion of the traditional structures of patriarchal repression. However, this is not something which comes out of the head. Before people can anticipate a liberated sexuality they need a society of abundance, which causes an efflorescence of desire; and they need also to have work restructured, so that women can begin to move independently as economic agents. And they need control over reproduction as well, so that sexual expression is not eternally complicated by the dependency of children. Technological advances in contraception and safe medical abortion are indispensable for this, but so are the social imperatives to keep families small. In the industrial nations, the necessity for a small family comes from the very high cost of raising children and from the fact that children are no longer producers when they are young (because production is automated), and providers for their parents when the latter are aged (because the state takes on this role with Social Security, and other similar measures). All of this weakens the influence of the church and other traditional centres of social control, which had enforced sexual repression.

These conditions are virtually non-existent in places like Nicaragua, where there is no abundance and the economy is largely pre-capitalist (Nicaragua barely has a proletariat, much less a major class of highly skilled professionals); where children are relatively inexpensive (the society being largely unaffected by consumerism) and often valued as producers for the family; and where there is no Social Security, very uncertain contraception, and a powerful Catholic church. All of this feeds into and is in turn organized by the myth of the Mother. The result is to put a value on the family which would gladden the heart of a right-wing Senator from Utah. The women's organization, AMNLAE, for example, states in their official set of propositions for the Constitution that the nuclear

107

family is the 'natural unit of society'. This is an astounding statement for an avowedly feminist organization – by North-american and European standards, that is.

One can readily tell apart the women *internacionalistas* from their Nicaraguan counterparts in Managua. The former declare they have broken free from the constraints of femininity, which are regarded as a denial of the female body, as defined and imposed by males. The latter meanwhile remain very much within the codes of traditional femininity, which also happen to be characteristics that separate the 'advanced' classes (that is those closer to the European model) from the common people. The problem has haunted every revolution and divided it internally: is it to be for the people, in their given state of development; or away from them, toward modernization? In Nicaragua, a Sandinista woman, highly radical in her political views, will take great pains to put on her makeup and shave under her arms. Though she wears the green military garb of the EPS or the Ministry of the Interior, there is still something 'ladylike' about her. She always wears a brassière, and is as much concerned to distance herself from peasant ways as she is to advance the Sandinist cause. The most femininely dressed women I saw in Nicaragua have been the members of AMNLAE. The sexuality of Nicaraguan women of the middle classes, whether inside or outside the revolution, often gives the impression of being trapped inside a bottle. There were as a result fewer liaisons between *internacionalistas* and Nicaraguans than I would have expected. A Mexican psychologist friend confided that he finds it too painfully difficult. Despite the closeness of the two Latin cultures, the sexual codes are too ambiguous and in the last analysis, too much out of phase.

ABORTION

It is not hard to see why the movement for women's rights stayed in narrow economic channels for the first years of the revolution, nor why, when it moved into the more open waters of sexuality itself, it encountered storms. And that these storms should be over the question of abortion is no mystery, either.

Ligia Altamirano is a young Nicaraguan obstetrician who has

recently completed her residency training programme. In the United States, resident physicians are trained not to speak unless spoken to; but Nicaragua is a country of and for the young, and its revolution was largely won by adolescents. I doubt whether a doctor of the old school would have bothered to do what Dr Altamirano did. But it is also true that the outrageous conditions she studied are, ironically enough, the product of the revolution.

Dr Altamirano works at the Berta Calderón Hospital, the only women's hospital in Nicaragua. She observed at first hand the horrible suffering and deaths of the women who came in with complications from illegal abortions; and she observed, too, that the cases seemed to be arriving with greater frequency. It was particularly disturbing to her that these women were those with the least risk of illness and obstetric complication – the healthy and the young. Worst of all was the realization that all the deaths and sterilizations – for many cases required hysterectomy to save the woman's life – were completely avoidable. This was no force of nature at work: it was the doing of men who had defined a culture and made laws controlling women's bodies and women's lives, laws that could put a poor woman in jail for four years if she had an illegal abortion – the illegality being an implication of the poverty, since an illegal abortion was one perforce chosen because of the hardship that another baby would bring. Well-to-do women in the same predicament could always pay for their illegal abortion and get it done with dispatch and hygienically. All that was needed was 40,000, 100,000, 200,000 córdobas, depending on the doctor and what the traffic would bear. Sometimes the doctor would even do the abortion in the public hospital, using the people's scarce resources for his own profit, and knowing that the authorities would look the other way.

This is scandalous under any circumstances; but in a revolution made for the poor, it becomes a shameful double outrage. And Dr Altamirano wrote it up, studying 109 cases in Berta Calderón who admitted to having illegal abortions. Obviously this was a minority of the total, since the illegality of an abortion means that one keeps quiet about it, indeed, only comes to the hospital as a last resort, and that is in the minority of instances in Nicaragua where a woman has access to the hospital at all; thus for every woman with

109

an illegal abortion who shows up at Berta Calderón, there must be many more suffering and dying silently in the countryside. Dr Altamirano found that most of these women had been pushed over the line of decision after abandonment by the father, that 55 percent had never tried any form of contraception, that the average cost to the health system of treating the complications of an illegal abortion was 96,571 córdobas, as against the cost of 150 córdobas for a therapeutic abortion (and 20 córdobas for the IUD, for which, of course, 'no hay') . . . and that ten of the women had died. This represented 27 percent of the deaths at Berta Calderón for the period of the study, March 1983 to November 1985.

By the time I interviewed Dr Altamirano in July 1986, another ten women had died. That the deaths would increase is only to be expected in view of the increasingly grave economic crisis of Nicaragua, and the ever greater number of women who are abandoned. (Which means – need we say? – that it is another cost to be put on the accounts of Mr Reagan's war.) There are a lot of frantic people in Nicaragua; and the thought of adding another child under such circumstances must seem increasingly intolerable. Even though the overall rate may not change very much, more of the women who are demanding abortions cannot afford the horrific prices charged by the private physicians. And so they put themselves at the most awful risk, then delay medical attention until it is too late, more out of fear of social condemnation than of the law.

Dr Altamirano presented her research at the third annual symposium between Northamerican and Nicaraguan health workers in November 1985, a highly visible event and just the right place to jog the Sandinist conscience. In any case, the findings from Berta Calderón had an explosive effect, and the story burst forth in *Barricada* on 19 November, under the headline: 'El Aborto: drama social que hay que solucionar' (Abortion: a social drama that has to be solved).

The abortion controversy may affect all the women of Nicaragua; but the abortion story which has been swept along on wings of compassion and moral outrage highlights the sufferings of its mothers. The very first article in *Barricada* had a picture of a sad-eyed nursing mother next to it; and a later story was headed

'Las madres muriendo' (the dying mothers). In the next three weeks, *Barricada* carried no less than nine pieces, some of them full-page, ruminating on every aspect of abortion in Nicaragua. There were round tables of professionals and of non-professionals, reflective essays on the taboo against sexual education and contraception, sharp reminders of the class bias inherent in the current situation and of the terrible guilt and shame poor women who have abortions are made to feel, reports of women who have had twelve children and no orgasms, heavy attacks on the venality and callousness of the medical profession, Marxist analyses of the history of anti-abortion legislation as a function of the demand for cheap labour, criticism of the Ministry of Health ('una burocracia atrasante y horrorosa' – backward and horrid), reminders that the *yanquis* with their Alliance for Progress had promoted sterilization campaigns against the Third World, and attacks on fathers who deserted the family and on the 'gran ignorancia que tienen los varones, que no saber nada de sexo, ni siquiera como se llaman los órganos sexuales y hasta se escandalizan cuando una los llama por su nombre científico', (the great ignorance of men, who know nothing about sex, not even the proper names for the sex organs, and are scandalized when the scientific name is used').

Almost all of the people cited were strongly in favour of changing the abortion laws, if not to legalize the practice then to 'depenalize' it (this being the position of the Oficina Legal de la Mujer). The only exceptions running against the current were the opinions of two male gynaecologists, one of whom termed himself a 'liberal'. He claimed that although Christian morality on the subject was false, abortion should be outlawed because Nicaragua was under-populated, a tragic fact obliging mothers to be fruitful; while the other felt that 'social changes' couldn't be solved through legislation, and that to do so would encourage 'impostors'.

And then, as suddenly as it had started, the campaign in *Barricada* ceased. No reasons were offered for the sudden loss of attention, but it is not difficult to imagine what they were. Months later I heard through a second-hand source that the people in the FSLN who decide such matters had elected to put the brakes on, because (to paraphrase) 'we can't get too far in front of the people'. From another angle, whatever immediate advantages may have been won in the effort to put through a more progressive social agenda in the face of the traditional resistance centring on the Catholic hierarchy had now been dissipated. The Right was counter-attacking on the cultural terrain which had always been its strongest ground, and scoring heavily.

It was apparent from the beginning that two quite distinct agendas were being woven together in the attack on the illegality of abortion: a sense of compassion and justice on the one hand, which could be articulated in the language of class oppression, and, on the other, a line of radical desire, epitomized in a quote from one of the articles – 'Las relaciones amoroso-sexuales son parte vital del amor que es por definición un valor revolucionario', (An erotic sexuality is part of love and is by definition a revolutionary value). In an ultimate sense, these two lines were both part of the revolutionary project. Nicaragua, however, is not an ultimate sense, but a very unevenly determined place, where different revolutionary agendas can conflict with each other. As we have seen, the latter strand is the province of the modernizing élites and, especially, the international-ists who have come to work for the revolution, bringing their First World values with them. It does not correspond to the sexual values and consciousness of the masses. As such, it is an issue made to order for the Nicaraguan Right, marching under the banner of the Catholic hierarchy.

The reaction was swift and fierce, in the right-wing *La Prensa*, which was to be expected, and even in the generally pro-Sandinista *Nuevo Diario*, which took a middle-of-the-road posture. The rights of the unborn were prominently featured, the soul being held to enter the foetus at conception. Abortion was strongly linked with free love and the moral dissolution of the North (a paradox, since it was even called a 'communist plot', prompting the reply that the US must therefore be a communist country). Mother Teresa was given repeated coverage, to show that a Catholic could have an 'option for the poor' and also say that 'those who destroyed the unborn, destroy God'. The FSLN was accused by the Conservative Party (which has billboards posted up in Managua proclaiming, 'La Familia es Conservatismo') of trying to wreck the Nicaraguan family by giving support to the legalization of 'uniones de hecho' (common-law marriages). The sayings of Pius XI were trundled out for viewing, along with the full panoply of opinion by the current Pontiff, for whom abortion is diabolism, pure and simple. Statements were made in *Nuevo Diario* that Nicaragua needed revolutionary solidarity and not the importation of ideology from bourgeois countries. Calls for population increase were heard. The reflection was made that just because robbery is inevitable as a result of poverty, we do not therefore legalize it. A woman named Mercedes Rodríguez de Chamorro made the interesting observation that to legalize abortion was the same as legalizing parricide, since the ranks of the unborn included future fathers. Irresponsibility was denounced ringingly in the pages of *La Prensa*. Finally, the film, *A Silent Scream*, which purports to depict the agony of a foetus being aborted, was described in hideous detail, as a kind of ultimate weapon against the godlessness of the revolution.

The abortion controversy was a godsend for the Right, providing an otherwise lacking bridge to the people. The Nicaraguan Right has no coherent social programme, and must live hand to mouth by promises of the prosperity which will return once Uncle Sam forgives Nicaragua its transgressions. Most of the alleged transgressions are of little concern to the average Nicaraguan. This cannot be said, however, about violations of the Word of God – and most Nicaraguans believe that abortion is just such a violation. They also fear further disintegration of their family structure, and mistrust the lasciviousness of the Northern nations. This sense is not confined to the Right, but affects the Church of the Poor as well, thus creating a serious confrontation between the two most dynamic groups of the revolution, women and radical Christians.

When I spoke to my friends in the liberation church about the abortion controversy, the atmosphere of discussion, usually so open and easy, would congeal. Pedro Joaquín Romero could be induced to admit that the problem was complex, but he hastened to underscore how different social conditions were in comparison to the North. One argument he advanced – and I must say it was the most spontaneous argument he advanced – was chillingly familiar. It was the cliché I had heard before, needless to add, from male lips: the nation is underpopulated; women should do their duty and

113

reproduce. This came forth during the visit of his brothers, as if to underscore that the three Romeros, otherwise so diverse politically and spiritually, were bonded together as men after all.

The Jesuit Peter Marchetti was considerably more forthcoming, but understandably more detached. Celibate men who live together and serve the Father should perhaps be excused from pronouncing on what is right for women to do. Of course few have taken this option. Marchetti, to his credit, stayed clear of pontification on the subject. He said instead what I should hope we all would say: that we should work for a society in which human beings can be human beings, and choices would not be put in Manichean terms; in other words, that we should create social conditions where women could be full moral agents. Well, that is no doubt so, but it doesn't say much about the here and now. As for that, Marchetti was critical of AMNLAE, saying that they were warring against the Nicaraguan bourgeoisie, which was fine as far as he was concerned, but ignored the deep opposition amongst the people, especially the peasantry. Peter claims that at a recent meeting of a base community in the north of Nicaragua, only one person of the hundred or so present seemed willing to even consider the depenalization of abortion – although a majority wanted better contraception. Unfortunately, better contraception won't silence the abortion question, any more than it has in the United States, where contraception is better than Nicaragua will achieve for fifty years, at least.

It might be added that when I reported Peter's doubts about the willingness of the people to contemplate changes in abortion policy to María de Zúñiga, she seemed not at all disturbed. After all, she told me, how do you expect the people to respond to a priest? This echoed what some of the leaders of the Oficina Legal da la Mujer said: that the people are divided inwardly on the matter, retaining respect for the teachings of the church, but deeply committed to changing their intolerable sexual condition. Recalling the compromise effected by the unmarried couple who decided to separate on their deathbed, it seemed to me that some solution which preserves the faith while giving women some control over their reproductive life was not out of the range of this ingenious people. After all, the Catholic doctrine on abortion is not, contrary to the impression given by John Paul II, actually engraved in stone. It, too, has a history, and can develop with the rest of the human species.

Perhaps the best word on this confrontation has been given by the redoubtable *El Tayacan*, in two issues of June, the month of the women's *cabildo*. The first, no. 193, was headlined 'Algo sobre el aborto' (Something about abortion), and had on its cover a photo of a beautiful young woman with a tear rolling down her cheek. Inside, under a lively cartoon depicting people in various stages of conflict about abortion, was an editorial. It described something of the different positions of the controversy, then came to the heart of the question. Abortion is never a good. Either it is an irresponsible decision or (in almost all cases) it is the last chapter in a sad history – because the mother is poor, because she is abandoned, because she is sick, because she cannot care for her child. 'Nunca ninguna mujer va a abortar como si fuera una fiesta, reclamando su derecho como una bandera de triunfo' (Never can any woman go to an abortion as if it were a party, claiming it as a right like a flag of triumph). Implicit here is the tragic sensibility which characterizes this noble journal. Abortion is not good, but may be necessary; and it should be freely chosen, one way or the other. The Constitution of the Nicaraguan people should guarantee 'el derecho a la libre reproducción' to the couple (the right of free reproduction), which means providing the basic tools and opportunities so that people can make a free choice, which may of course be the tragic choice of abortion.

These tools are often somewhat facilely summarized to feature sexual education, as if a few courses in sexuality would suffice, when what is demanded is to become capable of bearing the existential burdens of being human. But this is what the revolution itself says when it proposes the goal (unfortunately in sexist terms) of creating the 'nuevo hombre'. The liberated sexuality which is the goal of revolution is a sexuality of freedom, not of an orgastic discharge at will. Since sexuality engages the Other (not just one's partner but all dependent others, including the unborn), its freedom cannot be encompassed except in moral and, finally, tragic terms. *El Tayacan* grasps this point perfectly, which is why it proposes to make the church face up to the choice of abortion, instead of promoting the infantilization and stunting of human possibility which has been the traditional business of the Catholic hierarchy.

115

The same logic holds politically. Abortion should be decriminalized: the state has no more right of setting the terms of such a solemn decision than the church.

Sexuality in Nicaragua may be a dreadful mess, but there is one compensating feature to it which may be worth the pain. And that is the fact that it is being actively determined. The public debate, and the coverage by the press, can be silly at times, but its overall level puts to shame our so-called advanced institutions. It is an example – I am reluctant to use the shopworn term – of democracy at work – of people making direct changes in their public lives, by themselves, without waiting on the authorities. After all, it was the women's *cabildo* which kicked the door open after the party decided to close it for a while lest the Right have too much of a weapon. And it is to the credit of *Barricada* for responding, and showing that a party-sponsored press can be genuinely open to the will of the people.

I should also say that I am going to miss the role of *La Prensa** in the debate, as repulsive as I found that unhappy newspaper. I am not going to miss *La Prensa* itself, which got what it deserved when it accepted money from the power that is bringing war and holocaust to Nicaragua, and otherwise played the role of Reagan's lackey. But I do miss the presence of a genuine independent newspaper in Nicaragua. Without a voice in print, even a foolish, wrong-headed voice, to say no to the prevailing power, public discourse – and politics generally – is going to be weakened in Nicaragua. And whatever else it was, the abortion controversy that raged in the Nicaraguan press was fun to read.

---

* The anti-government newspaper *La Prensa* was shut down in June 1986 following the passage of $100 million in contra aid by the US Congress. *La Prensa* was reopened in late 1987 as part of the Arias Peace Plan.

5

PUERTO
CABEZAS

THE PLANE from Managua to Puerto Cabezas often flies due
east to Bluefields, then turns sharply north, hugging the
ruler-straight coast. I think they do this to avoid contra
ground-to-air fire; or perhaps the pilot enjoys the scenery. It is as if
God took a paintbrush soaked in green and laid it straight along the
ocean. Occasionally I saw little drops that must have been lagoons,
but for the rest it was a stark expanse of verdure separated by the
white line of the beach from the eternal sea. Mangrove swamp, I
suppose. There is nothing suggesting the handiwork of human
beings from this height – not a road, nor sign of a settlement. Just
flat green, blue, and that line of white.

The clouds had pulled back for the bulk of the flight, but as we
approached Puerto Cabezas they closed in, and the green and blue
world became grey. This must be the rain, I thought, the rain of the
rainy season on the Caribbean coast, the effortless and unending
rain of the tropics. Managua is wet, too, this time of year; but the
rain is episodic. It comes and goes. In Puerto Cabezas, the rain of
the rainy season seems forever. It does not come down from the
sky: it is the sky – 'For the rain it raineth every day'.

The puddles were calf-deep in the streets of Puerto Cabezas, and
in the small yard in front of the Comité Regional of the FSLN,
where I had been directed by the stocky and dour officer from the
Ministry of the Interior. He had picked me up slogging into town

from the airport, and taken me to his command post, where my papers, already damp from the rain, were examined and approved. I had expected him. 'You will always be watched in Puerto Cabezas', Freddy Balzan had said. 'Remember, it is a war zone. They will treat you well, but don't ever try going off on your own without telling them.' I had no intention of disobeying. Besides, how could one disobey in that fishbowl?

The letter of introduction was from Freddy to Subcomandante José González, chief of the FSLN for the province of Zelaya Norte, and thus for all intents and purposes, the Governor-General of north-eastern Nicaragua. González presides over the process of negotiating autonomy for the Miskitu Indians who live in this harsh region of swamp and salt flat. It would be hard to think of a more delicate and taxing job. The revolution has taken a major beating in the court of world opinion over its relations with the Indians. It is the one area in which mistakes are the most freely admitted; the one area where their fragile synthesis could become the most readily unstuck – and the one area most likely to be pounced upon by the enemy to the North. Everybody expects Nicaragua to be invaded through the capital of Zelaya Norte, Puerto Cabezas. After all, Puerto Cabezas was where Uncle Sam launched his boats for the Bay of Pigs back in 1961. He should know the place well, indeed, he watches it day and night looking for tears in the social fabric while doing what he can to make them happen.

And an intricate fabric it is. The Miskitus are divided into more factions than one can count, representing every shade of opposition and loyalty to the revolution, and they form the most active and politically aware element of Zelaya Norte. Yet the Miskitus are a minority, comprising about 75,000 of the 250,000 inhabitants of the region. Mestizos, many with Indian blood, are actually the largest fraction of the population, along with a sizeable contingent of Caribbean creoles, primarily Afro-American in culture, and other Indian tribes, the Sumos and Ramas, each with their own interests. All these peoples and more are scattered across this odd tableland of half water and half scrub, near-roadless and forsaken were it not for its strategic importance.

González is in charge here. It was he who, back in 1983, had the startling idea of talking to the Miskitus, to break out of the stalemate of hostility and suspicion. After a tense discussion among the revolution's leaders, permission was granted, and José, 'Chepe', González, with a few companions, set out in a jeep into Indian territory. They got out at the camp of the enemy, put their weapons down and said it would be better to talk than fight about the differences which divided the Miskitus and the Sandinistas. The gamble worked, and today González is alive and the regional chief of the FSLN. And I was going to see him, thanks to Freddy Balzan.

Freddy Balzan is an expansive and somewhat choleric Venezuelan, who helped the Sandinistas from his homeland when they were struggling for power, and threw his lot in with them after the triumph of the insurrection. He edits the journal, *Soberanía* (Sovereignty), which relentlessly bashes the United States for its attacks against Nicaragua and its intervention in the Third World. Freddy had been my fixer in Nicaragua, and it was to him I returned when my original efforts to get to Puerto Cabezas had stalled in the quicksand of the bureaucracy. I had been ashamed to tell Freddy of my frustration and failure, but he drew the information out of me, and in his impulsive way, immediately came up with a new and better idea.

'Listen, there is an FAS plane leaving next Saturday morning. Be at the kiosk opposite the Exxon station near the airport at 6.30. You will have reservations going out, and returning next Tuesday – though don't be upset with me if the plane can't come back. We have "gran tormentas", hurricanes, plus sometimes the planes don't work, and you know we have no parts. You will need a letter for the Immigration, in Puerto Cabezas, it will help you.' And he disappeared into the back of his offices, sacred ground where I was forbidden to enter, emerging ten minutes later with a formal note addressed to González, which identified me as a friend to Nicaragua and a writer, and asked that all good auspices be given me. Freddy asked me to repeat my instructions, and when he was satisfied that my dim Spanish had absorbed his message and that I absolved him in advance in case I never returned, he certified that all was well with a resounding '¡Cor-r-r-recto!' and added: 'Now you are all set. And the only thing I want you to bring back is four pounds of shrimp.'

All set. I was going to have an insider's tour, all expenses paid, of the most sensitive zone of the revolution. Freddy was a personal friend of Tomás Borge, at the top of the authority chain in Nicaragua. Freddy was friend to my friends Ellen and Bill, which made me friends with Freddy, and through him, with the great Borge. I was on the side of the power now, no longer estranged as at home. Moreover, I was, one would have to say, ideologically reliable. Mere friendship, even gratitude for the carton of Marlboros I had brought him as a gift, would not have induced Freddy to put himself out to get me to Puerto Cabezas. He would have to expect that something of value for the revolution would come out of my visit. It would be an exchange, a fair deal: I give Freddy some Marlboros, Freddy – and Borge – give me a first-class trip to Puerto Cabezas, and I give them back a favourable report.

When I told Peter H the news, he was furious, with the injured idealism of the young. 'Damn it! That's just what's wrong with this place! You only get something on the basis of who you know. It's one great big clique.' Poor boy, I thought. His frustrations with the cronyism in his office must be getting him down. But I responded with heated defensiveness: 'How in hell do you expect them to choose somebody? You know what they're up against. Do you think they should have a lottery to see who goes to Puerto Cabezas? Or why don't they try affirmative action, and send a CIA man? Two flights a week, no roads, a war zone. They have to know who they're dealing with. This is the only way they can take care of themselves.'

It was an easy argument to win, and I found myself going over it mentally as I waited in the kiosk across from the Exxon station two mornings later. A slender woman with an olive complexion called my name, and I ran to get my pack and into the line. The FAS (Fuerza Aérea Sandinista) plane stood on the runway, a sturdy twin-engine cargo aircraft of British extraction attended by youths in olive-drab, some ticking off names listed on clipboards. Before we took our places on the benches running lengthwise along each side of the fuselage, we had to wait for the bay to be filled with its cargo. A truck pulled up, loaded with oblong pale green wooden boxes. One by one, the young men took them off and placed them in the bay of the plane. They were coffins, coffins for Puerto Cabezas.

THE SUBCOMANDANTE

I was surprised to learn how young Puerto Cabezas was. Originally a Sumo Indian village, the site was occupied sometime in the past century by the more aggressive Miskitu. Then the lumber and mining companies of the interior, enterprises with names like Baccaro Brothers and Bragman Bluff and Lumber, along with the ubiquitous United Fruit, decided they needed a port to get their commodities out of the region and into the world market. Because there is no natural harbour along this stretch of coast, the corporations built a jetty, first in 1918, and again in the 1930s, after Somoza took power. They built it of wood, in the cheapest and flimsiest way possible, being concerned only that the jetty last as long as it took them profitably to extract the region's natural resources. The agreeable Somoza let them do it without demanding any compensation in exchange, so that the town which arose about the jetty and became named Puerto Cabezas grew without any lasting infrastructure, nothing that is, of concrete or such material as could withstand the brutal humidity. The corporations calcu- lated well, as they always do. By the 1960s, the land had been sucked dry and made barren. The corporations could no longer extract their profit from Puerto Cabezas, and departed abruptly, leaving as memories of their presence a rotting wharf and a teetering collection of ramshackle wooden shacks.

The town has prematurely aged, less from the climate than from neglect, which exposes lifeless materials to the accelerated katabol- ism of the tropics and turns the works of human hands into fantastic spectacles of decay. Of course this makes Puerto Cabezas 'colourful'. If one is tired of freeway and shopping-mall culture, of high technology and a surfeit of glossily wrapped commodities, of the manipulations of television, and of the distractions of wealth and materialism in general, then I can firmly recommend a voyage to Puerto Cabezas, for there are none of these things there. There is one traffic light, at a corner of the little overgrown town square, where the dirt road from the interior meets the right-angled and wide sandy streets of the town; but this functions more as a gesture than a regulator of traffic. There is of course some traffic – Puerto Cabezas is not, after all, one of those villages where dogs sleep in the middle of the road – but considering that the population is twenty thousand, its streets are as little travelled as can be. And although it is an outpost, Puerto Cabezas is no frontier town, intruded upon by wilderness, but a very gentle place, full of the signs of society, and full of people, too, especially around evening, when the impossible buildings which appear to have been reduced to stacks of splinters by the elements discharge their inhabitants into the road.

Yes, the elements. The Comité Regional of the FSLN for Zelaya Norte must be the only administrative nerve centre in the world surrounded by tadpoles, hundreds of whom could be observed cavorting in the moat-like puddles as I crossed the makeshift bridge between the low yellow building and the street. Entering, I found myself in a small and crowded antechamber which served as a reception area and opened onto a larger waiting area for the bank of offices where the Sandinistas carried out their transactions. The reception area was the place to be identified and get prepared suitably for the business at hand, as spelled out by a scrawled sign posted over the desk: 'Cros: favor pedir permiso antes de pasar. Los que portan armas dejarlos en la RECEPCIÓN.'*

I surrendered Freddy's letter to the young woman behind the desk and waited. A flicker of recognition: 'Ah yes, you are the writer come from Managua. We have been expecting you. Compañera Yvonne will see to your needs while you are here. Yvonne! Ah, here she is.' I turned and faced the slender olive-complexioned woman who had called my name at the airport in Managua. Yvonne Rodríguez was her name, and she was twenty-four, half-Miskitu and mother of two, from the sacred Río Coco that divides Nicaragua from Honduras. She was my chaperone, reserved, efficient, and tolerant of poor Spanish. Her job was to see that a visitor to Puerto Cabezas was properly treated and formed a good impression of the revolution. Now that we had formally met, Yvonne's first task was to tell me that the Subcomandante would see me that day, but a little later, as he was in a meeting. Meanwhile, we would get organized. I would be shown my rooms

---

* Comrades: please ask permission before entering. Leave your weapons at the reception desk.

and the place where my meals were to be taken, the 'Comedor Marbella'. Perhaps I would like a coffee, or some *fresco*, after my trip. Of course, not much would be open, it being nine-thirty in the morning, but we could try.

The rain had relented; and so we set off for downtown Puerto Cabezas, over the swarms of tadpoles, past the Bragman movie theatre with its announcement in chalk, and into the little overgrown square with a tank with flat tyres at one corner and the lazy traffic signal at another. My quarters were by the sea, in a large tin-roofed house on stilts, one of a number built before the revolution to serve as dwellings for workers. All the houses save the guest house of the FSLN were at present occupied by extremely poor and evidently unemployed people, many displaced by the upheavals which had doubled the population of the town in the last five years. It was ironic to see these exemplars of Third World poverty living on a scenic bluff overlooking the fabulous Caribbean Ocean. I recalled rumours that the revolution had been approached by the insatiable resort industry to open up a stretch of the beautiful coast for the enjoyment of wealthy gringos. Did these people muse upon the potential value of their scenery as they sat there, surrounded by children and dogs?

The Comedor Marbella proved to be a shapeless house along the main street, motley grey, blue and brown like almost all the other houses in Puerto Cabezas, and with a large, high-ceilinged front room that served as the public dining room, the family's living room, and a recreation area for the children. A muscular young man was dribbling a basketball around a two-year-old as I was introduced to the proprietress, and the baby's squeals of delight served as a counterpoint to the woman's lament: 'Aie, it is a bad time to come to Puerto Cabezas. No hay nada, ni cebollas ni cerveza ni gaseosa.' To be out of onions is bad enough. But to be without beer or soda . . . how could the people endure it? It is very hard, admitted Yvonne. Almost all the food comes in by boat, but the disintegrating pier is being repaired and shipments can be made only two weeks of every month. The boat comes by way of Bluefields, which means that the contras are able to create some havoc with the shipments. Almost nothing works now, because of the poverty, the worthless infrastructure inherited from the

123

multinationals who pulled out, and above all, the war. Thanks to international aid, a good water system was opened in 1982, but the contras destroyed it, just as they destroy all the phone lines leading out of the town; and now Puerto Cabezas can return to the ranks of water-starved tropical towns inundated by torrential rains. Somehow we get through, said Yvonne, but it is *duro, muy duro*.

It was also *duro* to get a refreshment at that hour, but we eventually managed, Yvonne insisting on picking up the tab, and made our way back to the Comité Regional, in a renewed downpour. I had now graduated to the inside waiting area, where I could sit in one of the rocking-chairs until the Subcomandante was able to receive me. There is not much to see in that waiting room. I listened to the drilling of the rain on the roof and studied the sternly idealistic posters. One was of the famous Santos López, the only man to have served both with Sandino and the FSLN, and the other of a man I had not heard of before, a Gabriel Bell, a community worker assassinated in his home by contras. Bell's image fascinated me. The portrait was drawn with no great skill, indeed, one would have to call it crude. Yet the face had the kind of serenity and radiance I had come to associate with a Piero della Francesca. It was clearly a case of inspiration.

And then, as suddenly as he had begun, José González reached went out to the Marbella for my first meal (not at all bad, despite the lamentation), and read and reread *Barricada*. Periodically Yvonne or one of her associates would enter to inform me that the Subcomandante had been delayed but was still intending to see me. People trooped through, some in uniform and some carrying side-arms despite the posted prohibition. A small swarthy fellow appeared now and then bearing an AK47 sub-machine-gun, looked intently about with his sharp eyes, and left as silently as he came. In fact, the only noise I heard for the bulk of that day was the subdued clatter of typewriters from the other side of the wall. Once the power failed for about an hour, producing some embarrassed looks and a general aura of resignation.

At length a tall young man came by dressed in camouflage fatigues and with a .45 pistol strapped to his belt. I had seen him earlier and took him for an adjutant or a security guard. But a closer look revealed four bars on each shoulder. It was Subcomandante González himself, smiling and apologizing, telling me that my wait would soon be over, and passing on into the inner recesses of his command post. I interpreted him to mean at least another hour, and settled down for one more reading of *Barricada*. Ninety minutes later I was ushered down a dimly lit corridor for the long-awaited interview with the Governor-General of north-eastern Nicaragua.

As I set up my tape recorder for the interview, my first thought was that González looked very fair and European, and awfully young for his age, no more than twenty-seven or so. In fact, he looked positively boyish. With his large frame, prominent, fleshy features, and exuberant manner, José González could be imagined as a young, clean-shaven Fidel Castro. He waited, smiling cherubically and quietly drumming his fingers on the desk, as I fumbled with the equipment and delivered my carefully prepared and lengthy opening question. I wanted González to know my concern about the negative press the Sandinistas had been given about the Miskitus, and how badly this had divided progressives in the United States. There was a significant fraction of the Left who considered the Sandinistas little more than another form of white imperialism bent upon crushing the independent spirit of the Indians and subsuming them into Greater Nicaragua. A good number of films, video documentaries and reportage had portrayed the Indians as Noble Savages being crushed yet once more by the modern state – and this barrage had had its effect. No doubt the US establishment was using the conflict as a wedge to be driven between the Sandinistas and their base of support, but there was no doubt, either, that there was something really there for them to exploit.

I was hoping to avoid a strident and dogmatic interview, especially as my feeble command of Spanish made it unlikely that the discussion could be recuperated if it got off to a poor start. But perhaps my Spanish was too feeble to have made myself clear in the first place, or perhaps González was just feeling like unwinding. In any case, after hearing me out languidly for a few minutes, he suddenly erupted. Where once had sat a smiling youngster who could pass for a camp counsellor, now spoke a hardened Party ideologue.

125

There is no antagonistic contradiction between the Indians and the Sandinistas, declaimed González. The only antagonistic contradiction is between Imperialism and both of us. We have different histories, but each is of a violent colonialism. The Indians were manipulated by the British, who colonized them, to be used against the Spanish, and we, who had suffered under the Spanish, learned to look down on the Indians. It is natural, then, that there would be some difficulty at first between the races, and indeed the FSLN made some errors in the beginning, the worst of which was to trust the Miskitu leader, Steadman Fagoth. But that is all behind us now. We are going to give the Indians autonomy, allowing them the free development of their lands and their own cultural expression. The Indian masses are backing us; and only counter-revolutionaries stand against this process.

He went on this way for fifteen or twenty minutes, running down the list of the various Miskitu factions he had to deal with, drawing my attention to an official booklet full of facts and figures (and several poorly focused photographs of himself, in his eternal military garb, standing amidst Miskitu warriors a head shorter and several degrees of colour darker than him), and reeling off other statistics as he went. It was all very informative, but no more so than reading the booklet in the first place, and except for the problem of translation, posed no challenge at all and taught me nothing I did not essentially know already. A wave of despair passed over me as I furiously scribbled trying to keep up with González's incantation. Was I wasting my time? Had I come all the way to this swamp of a place, this Macondo at the end of the world, just to be harangued by someone who looked scarcely older than my own son? How could I express to González that these slogans were not what I was interested in hearing, that I wanted rather somehow to come into contact with the lived experience of revolution in the north-eastern corner of Nicaragua?

And then, as suddenly as he had begun, José González reached over and shut off the tape recorder. 'Bastante' – enough – he said, and his face sagged and suddenly flooded with fatigue. 'Es duro ser revolucionario', he said vacantly. He thought for a moment, then added with a flicker of energy, 'pero tengo fe en el poder del pueblo.

Soy optimista.'* I replied that this faith of his was a precious thing, and that the young people today in the US, of my own children's generation, lacked such faith and were often cynical. They were cowed by the nuclear weapons and had been made to feel that nothing could really change. González wanted to know how old my children were, and I said the older ones ranged into the early twenties.

'Yo,' he said, pointing to himself, 'soy veintesiete . . . y trece años en la revolución Sandinista.' So his looks did not deceive. The Governor-General of Northern Zelaya, the military commander-in-chief of the region and the man charged with negotiating the FSLN into peace with the Miskitu Indians and depriving the US of its prime opportunity of destroying the revolution from within, was twenty-seven. His life had been the revolution since the age of fourteen. At an age when my children were doing book reports in high school José González was organizing for the *Frente* in his native Matagalpa. And while they were hanging out and listening to heavy metal rock, he had been in the mountains living like an animal and building the revolution. His great-grandfather had been a fighter with Sandino, and his grandfather an anti-Somoza activist. Of his ten brothers and sisters, one fell during the insurrection, and one lived privately. The other eight all worked in one capacity or another for the FSLN, though none quite so prominently as José.

He paused and stared ahead, then down at my dormant tape recorder and the pen lying beside it. 'Y esto,' he said, taking the pen in his hand and waving it about with a flourish, 'esto es su arma.' He handed me the pen – my 'weapon' – and arose, announcing that he had to go out now, to attend an 'acto', and that I was welcome to accompany him. He called out, and the small swarthy man with the sub-machine-gun materialized from behind the door where he had been waiting. He was Felipe, a Miskitu bodyguard and chauffeur to the Subcomandante, and he never left González's side for the remainder of the evening.

---

* It is hard to be a revolutionary . . . but I have faith in the power of the people. I am an optimist.

As we scrambled for the door it suddenly occurred to me that never before in my stay in Nicaragua had I been in such danger as under the protective AK47 of Felipe. There was nothing ceremonial about these weapons. Here I was with two seriously armed men, heading toward a smart-looking Toyota Jeep which was going to take me for a drive along the now teeming streets of Puerto Cabezas, a town which must contain any number of people with an interest in eliminating my host in a hail of gunfire. How could the FSLN, with all their vigilance, keep assassins from infiltrating the town? And how would the assassin's bullet know not to include me in its itinerary?

The rains had cleared and the late afternoon sky was scrubbed pink and cast a soft light over the streets and rickety buildings. It seemed as if someone ran from every corner and every doorway to greet the Subcomandante. This brought the pace of the Jeep to a walk – not a bad idea in view of the condition of the washboard-like road, but not conducive to my sense of security. However it seemed that González could not resist the crowd. At first I wondered if it were for my consumption, this gladhanding and backslapping and first-naming, this extravagant and cheerful display of face-to-face politics, tending to the mother of Manuel and Chepita's licence and the broken bridge in front of Rosario's house and the composition of that night's vigilance. But how could it be? How, that is, could this have been some kind of Potemkin village, all the citizenry artfully arranged for the benefit of the foreign correspondent, giving on subtle command their demonstration of civic unity with the leadership of José González? I suppose it might have been logically possible, but not in Nicaragua, land of 'no hay' and 'no se encuentra', never.

Eventually we arrived at the site of the 'Acto', a spacious and canopied structure in the grounds of a convent. It was Puerto Cabezas' High School; and we were to attend a graduation ceremony – a kind of landmark in the development of the revolution on the Atlantic coast. There were some sixty neatly dressed young people on one side of the auditorium, with their families on the other, and a small number of dignitaries and officials on the dais. While Felipe waited by the door, José González and I mounted the stage to take our seats among the establishment.

I heard my name being read by a slender young man and the applause of the audience. It was a flowery introduction, in a formal and elevated Spanish, puzzling at first, until I recognized the cadences of Freddy Balzan's prose. González had passed along my letter of introduction, which proclaimed to the assembly my virtue and revolutionary solidarity. I had become drafted into the élite of Puerto Cabezas, and I was going to be awarding these young people their diplomas. Though González had started explaining it to me on the trip from the Comité Regional, the nature of the school remained obscure. As if in answer to my puzzlement, a woman on the dais passed a small sheet of paper on which was scrawled in pencil the following: 'We are an indians school. we teach bilingual, in spanish and miskitu.'

The students trooped to the dais to receive their diplomas and prizes, to receive our congratulations and to sing Miskitu songs. They could have passed for an inner-city high school graduating class – until their hands, roughened by rural life, were shaken. The Miskitu have a very strong sense of identity, but this is not reflected in the kind of distinctive dress and appearance seen, for example, in the Indians of Guatemala. A newcomer would be hard put to distinguish the average Miskitu from the Latino population of Nicaragua.

As the shyly smiling youngsters came, one by one, to receive our benediction, I was able to piece together some more of what the school was about. It was a new project of the revolution, and this was its first graduating class. The students themselves were being trained as teachers. They came by boat from all over the province, from as far as 100 kilometres away, and lived on the premises for six months. Then they returned to their communities and took up the task of bilingual teaching and revolutionizing their people. The point was underscored in González's commencement address, delivered haltingly at first in clumsy Miskitu and then in a fiery and ceremonial Spanish. They were there to learn 'ciencia', to get strength from knowledge, to overcome the prejudices of the past, and, ultimately, to become the 'nuevos hombres' of the revolution. He saluted their courage in coming to the school in the face of the imperialist aggression which threatened them. Then he turned in my direction, citing me, to laughter and applause, as a North-

american 'amigo de la humanidad',* who was here to study the
revolutionary development of the peoples of the Atlantic coast. And
he told them how proud he was that I was able to see such a fine
group of young men and women.

The time had come to end the 'Acto', and the familiar tune of the
Sandinista anthem was heard. I listened for the customary sounds
of 'Adelante marchemos compañeros . . .' (Forward we march,
comrades), but heard instead a strange and gutteral collection of
syllables, sounding to my untrained ear like 'wicky wacky wookie'.
If the words were unrecognizable, the language could not be
mistaken. I was hearing the Sandinista hymn sung in the tongue of
the Miskitu Indians who were supposed to be the mortal enemies of
the revolution.

Afterwards we drifted outside while González held court, the
ever-present Felipe sitting nearby in the Toyota, AK47 in his lap.
My Spanish breaks down completely when I am listening to the
colloquial conversation of others, and so I could make nothing of
what was being said beyond the fact that it appeared to be the
source of general amusement. In fact, all sense of hierarchy seemed
to have dissolved. If one could abstract the camouflage fatigues
with the four shoulder stripes, the .45 pistol and the bodyguard, the
group could have been a collection of young loafers discussing a
football match. From another perspective, it was as if the Governor
of California, George Deukmejian, was horsing around with some
street people from Watts. The conversation drifted onward,
punctuated by one, then another brief power failure, each leaving
us in utter darkness. These are scarcely worth commenting upon in
Nicaragua, though three in a day struck me as a bit much, and these
latter two gave my heated imagination fuel for anxious ruminations
on the opportunity they afforded for terrorists to strike down the
architect of peace between the Indians and the Sandinistas as he
cracked jokes and clowned around with the townspeople.

At length the conversation ran its course. The Subcomandante
turned to me and asked if I wanted to go dancing. '¿Cómo no?' –

* The allusion is to the famous line of the Sandinista anthem, in which the
people are exhorted to struggle against 'el yanqui, enemigo de la humanidad'
(the enemy of humanity).

why not? – I responded gamely, but he seemed to forget the offer as soon as it was made, and immediately shifted the topic to food and his need thereof. Off we went in the Toyota, Felipe at the wheel and González bantering with the citizenry as before. We drove out of the more populous district and onto a quiet and dimly lit road. After about half-a-mile, the Toyota turned into a short driveway and paused before a gate. A soldier materialized and opened the gate, and we passed into a well-lit compound of approximately half an acre in area, surrounded by a cyclone fence. A modest house stood in the middle; an elderly woman sat rocking on the porch with a beautiful young girl asleep in her lap. José greeted her warmly and introduced me. Inside, everything was plain but well-laid out. It reminded me of a bungalow in the Adirondacks. González proudly showed me a photo of his wife and two children, temporarily away in Managua. He indicated an alcove off the kitchen where I could spend the night. I declined – foolishly, it turned out – because all my possessions were stowed at the guest house next to the sea. Meanwhile the woman had put the child to bed and fetched us our dinner, a plate full of hard-boiled eggs, tortillas, and the ubiquitous *fresco*.

As we ate, and for an hour afterwards, José González continually plied me with questions about life in the United States. Did people there like this song, which was a favourite of his? He began to sing me a few lines: 'We are de worruld / we are de peopul . . .', then broke off and hummed the rest. Ah, that is a good song, very popular in Nicaragua. (Indeed it was; they played it at ear-splitting volume at the sixth anniversary celebration of the revolution.) There are so many good things about the United States, it's too bad the government is so bad, he went on, then turnë to his ignorance of the English language. Now that's what I want to learn, said González, and asked me if I had a dictionary handy. I extracted my faithful and indispensable *New World Spanish/English–English/Spanish Dictionary*, its yellow and red paper cover and 1226 EASY-TO-READ PAGES frayed and curling, and passed it over. He began to leaf through it, turning the pages at random and choosing such words as caught his eye. He would read the Spanish and then try to pronounce the English while I hovered nearby and did my best to help his pronunciation. 'Tornado', 'topcoat', 'brain', 'derange' . . .:

131

he practised each word until the sound became recognizably English. Then with a kind of omnivorous curiosity, he would attempt to understand the word, would play with it like a kitten with a ball of wool until he felt it was his. The Governor-General of Northern Zelaya was allowing himself to be the schoolboy he never had been.

We must have done thirty or forty words in this fashion, with only one interruption. A rustling noise outside caught González's attention. He motioned me to be quiet and moved softly to the door, hand moving up near the holster on his right hip. Softly he opened the door, peered outside into the mild night air, then returned to resume his lesson. And then, as suddenly as it began, the lesson ended. Face clouded over with exhaustion, José González slumped in his chair and pronounced the day over. Felipe was called, we exchanged parting good wishes, and my visit with the subcomandante came to an end. It was nine o'clock in the evening.

A DIFFICULT NIGHT

Felipe jabbered away in an unrecognizable dialect during the return trip to my quarters, while I politely pretended to understand and tried to sort out the impressions of the day. But when we came to the house on stilts overlooking the sea, my attention was abruptly diverted by a physical fact of over-riding urgency: the fourth power failure of the day had descended over Puerto Cabezas, or at least this district of it, and my quarters were in total darkness. This was no joke. I was alone now, having decided it would be unmanly to return with Felipe; I had no light and only a very hazy idea of the layout of the guest house; and there was no other place to go in the darkened town.

I had allowed myself to take a coffee with González as we reviewed the English language together, and was not the least bit sleepy. But what else was there to do except to sleep? Nothing but make the best of it. I stumbled up the stairs and felt my way along the wooden walls, tripping and bumping into unseen objects until I came to my room, found my pack, fumbled about in it and made myself ready for bed. Having been told that Puerto Cabezas was a haven for mosquitoes, I had purchased in Managua a device known as KIN KON, named for the fearsome ape whose portrait decorated the package. The product itself consisted of a little spiral made of some kind of punky substance, which when burned was supposed to give off fumes to deter the little beasts. I decided to use KIN KON – if only to create a speck of light – and managed to locate my supply in the pocket of my pack, along with a box of matches I had providently taken along. I was now beginning to feel almost pleased at this demonstration of human sensory skill, forethought and ingenuity marshalled against the dumb forces of nature. I had only to light the match and a sense of mastery, if not comfort, would be mine.

I had forgotten that the matches were of Nicaraguan manufacture, which is to say, made with a papery shaft and other substances that hygroscopically lap up the Puerto Cabezas humidity. I might as well have tried to get sparks from a wet noodle as from one of those matches. I recalled Omar Cabezas's description in *Fire from the Mountain* of how the guerrillas made fires in the rain; but no act of the imagination could instil in me such an adaptation to the forces of the tropics. I was, and would remain irrevocably, a gringo in the dark, like a Fay Wray without KIN KON, in a god-forsaken town awaiting Yankee invasion, and at the mercy of the creatures of the night.

The bed was thin and narrow, and reminded me of my cot back at Pedro Joaquín Romero's house. Surprisingly, the mosquitoes held off; perhaps the stiff off-shore breeze detained them. Still, I felt vaguely uneasy as I lay in the dark. I had climbed into bed with the intention of trying to think through the vivid experiences of the day, indeed, of meditating upon the whole buzzing and blooming confusion of the Sandinista revolution. But my vague discomfort crowded out other thoughts. Instead of offering a safe place for contemplation, the darkness and isolation seemed to be forcing me inward, toward hypochondria and melancholy ... and in the course of time, to sleep.

I awoke bolt upright into total blackness. There was no way of knowing how long I had slept, nor was I the least bit interested in the fact. All I knew was that something was drastically wrong. As the higher centres of my brain came on line, it became possible to say where, if not why. My legs seemed to be on fire. Nothing vague about this discomfort: what I was experiencing now below each knee was clearly heir to the unease I had felt before dropping off to sleep. I felt as if plunged up to my knees in hell, and my lower extremities were to pay for all the crimes of the world. If this were a torture session with the Salvadorean Treasury Police, I think I would have confessed to anything. But there was no one to confess to, no way of knowing what was torturing me, and no way of bringing it to an end – though instinct rid me immediately of the bed and drove me, stumbling and cursing, into the front room, where I found my way to one of the cracked naugahyde chairs and fell in a twitching heap.

As I writhed about, I became dimly aware of a dim, rhythmical sound amid the soughing of the breeze, the creaking of the shutters and the squeaking of my chair. Shades of Queequeg! Somebody was asleep in a neighbouring chair . . . I was in Nicaragua and in Nicaragua one is never alone.

His name was Alvaro, and he was a thin old man with a straggly beard and a wispy voice, employed by the Party as a night-watchman for their guest house. I learned this later, after some hours of lonely agony. My legs grew no worse, and indeed I seemed to become habituated to the itching; but with the dying of the breeze, mosquitoes arrived to liven things up. They must have awakened Alvaro, who announced himself by cursing the 'zancudos'. We struck up a conversation, the subject of KIN KON was broached, and I decided to have another go at igniting this mysterious agent, using for the purpose another pack of matches. Miraculously, the second pack worked. I do not know what mosquitoes find obnoxious about KIN KON, which is a rather pleasant-smelling substance so far as I am concerned. In any event, seeing the dull glow of the smouldering end was reassuring. It was a harbinger of the dawn I now craved and a reminder that we humans were not totally helpless against nature.

Slowly, ever so slowly, dawn crept into that room, and as the light advanced, my pain retreated. It became light enough to make out the features of Alvaro, and then light enough to return to the scene of the crime. Who had been my exotic torturer? The bedroom with its dark blue walls and pink closets appeared innocent enough, and nothing seemed amiss save the rumpled bedclothes. I tore the bed apart, looking for signs of the enemy, and found nothing. Then I paused and stared at the sheets. Tiny creatures were traversing the expanse of cotton, like commas in motion on a white page. They were reddish and not very exotic looking at all. Indeed, they were ants, the most common animals in all the world – though perhaps not all are like the type that dwells in Puerto Cabezas and eats the flesh of gringos.

'¡Hormigas!' I called out to Alvaro, who came and clucked sympathetically. Later I said the same in a more demanding and complaining tone (for I had resolved never to spend another night in that literal hellhole until the problem was solved) to Rosa, the young woman assigned to clean the quarters and take care of them during the day. The beads of sweat on her upper lip budged not at all as she heard me out impassively, and reminded me that it was Sunday, in other words, 'ahorita, no hay nada', and that 'mañana' she could get some Pinasol and solve all the problems posed by the hormigas. 'Hay una noche hasta mañana', I said ominously, but Rosa only shrugged.

THE GREAT DISILLUSIONMENT

As I walked to the Comité Regional, the solution to the hormiga problem occurred to me in a flash: simply wear one's socks to bed, tuck one's trouser legs under them, and let the ants be damned. The idea lightened my spirits, and got the morning's sightseeing off to a good start. I was to be driven about by a very dark-skinned young Miskitu named Fernando, in a shapeless Toyota pick-up truck sans windshield, with Yvonne and one of her sons in the rear. We could go anywhere, within reason and the capability of the Toyota, which turned out to be marginal. There were no electrical power failures that day, but the truck made up for it on four occasions by needing a push start. In fact, it soon became clear that the engine lacked the capability of starting on its own altogether. This required that it be kept running at all times, though even so it would stall. In true Nicaraguan spirit, there was much hilarity about the pathetic condition of the poor vehicle, as well as good exercise in the pushing. All in all, it was a jolly morning.

135

We visited the nearby Miskitu hamlet of Komla, driving through a landscape of scrub pine and salt flat punctuated by numerous lookout towers of the Sandinista army. Convoys of laughing soldiers would pass in either direction, and fortifications or camps seemed to lie beyond every hillock. Little communities of Indians live amidst this scene. These are people with no visible economy, their huts strewn across the ungiving land. There is an occasional pig, but no gardening to speak of. Once they could fish, but the war has severely limited that, and now they live on handouts, which means at the edge of starvation.

It being Sunday, a service was underway in the small chapel, conducted in the Moravian faith imported for the Indians by the British many generations ago. The service goes on for three or four hours at a stretch, which may seem an inordinate amount of time to us, but is quite reasonable for people who live in places like Komla, where there are not many distractions, to say the least. In a remarkable display of cultural syncretism, the Indians have adopted as their patron saint the medieval Czech martyr, Jan Hus. It turned out we had arrived on the anniversary of Hus's death in the year 1437. The deacon – if that is what he is called – commemorated the event with a very long and instructive discourse on Hus, emphasizing his defiance of the corrupt authority of the Pope, and the sufferings which befell him as a result.

It was an amazing scene. Here, in a little makeshift chapel on a near-treeless plain in north-eastern Nicaragua, was a Miskitu Indian talking of an Eastern European martyr to a white man whose ancestors fled Eastern Europe and Russia, the Indian retelling a tale told to his people by English imperialism, of an older, Holy Roman imperialism, for the purposes of calling attention to a rival Catholic–Spanish imperialism; and the scion and negation of this are the Sandinistas, who are ambiguously in the position of imperialist to the Indians, while they themselves struggle against the Yankee imperialism which succeeded both English and Spanish imperialism and against which the white man was himself trying to struggle. This bizarre tapestry was woven in the threads of three languages: Miskitu, Spanish and English. I could see myself in it peering out from behind now one, now another, of its figures. Was I, too, being lived by this history? Or was I living it?

Later Yvonne and Fernando dropped me off in town and went their private ways. I passed a desultory and lonely afternoon tramping about town, visiting the dilapidated jetty, and swimming in the warm and murky Caribbean. I felt the ennui of the tropics, the emptiness of its days and the endlessness of its heat . . . and the forlornness of Puerto Cabezas, more, its exhaustion. Puerto Cabezas, mellow and funky in retrospect, can in its somnolent presence seem to be on the lip of an abyss. After supper at the Marbella, I planned to take in the movie at the Bragman Theatre, mostly for sociological reasons; but after a few turns around the darkened town square, the idea no longer seemed appealing. Perhaps it was the meal, the first greasy and disagreeable one of the tour, working on me. It seemed an age since the hectic tour with González; now I was a cipher, drifting aimlessly. I made my way back to the guest house, not knowing what to do with the evening, and hoping to see the familiar face of Alvaro.

But Alvaro was not there. Another man was in his place, Diego, a Mestizo who served as the alternate watchman. He was squarely built, younger than Alvaro and garrulous. I took heart. Here was a fine, informal opportunity to get to know one of the ordinary folk of Puerto Cabezas. How nice: I would have a chat with Diego. We had plenty of time and nothing to do but talk. Of course, I reasoned, this Diego was probably a Party man, rewarded by the FSLN for his loyalty with this cushy job where all he had to do was pass three nights a week at the guest house being nice to guests of the Party and reassuring them about the Revolution. However, I could allow for these distortions.

I am not sure exactly what I expected to hear, but it was not what I got. No sooner asked about life in Puerto Cabezas, Diego, as if programmed by Ronald Reagan's speech-writers, launched into a bitter denunciation of the Sandinistas. Once we had a good life here, he said. You could go into the stores and buy anything you wanted. The shelves were full of all kinds of good things from the States, good clothes, transistor radios, and plenty of good liquor to drink. Nobody bothered you and you could do anything you wanted.

137

He continued: Then these communists came, and now there is nothing to eat. The price of meat has gone up to four times what it was a year ago. Nobody can afford any meat, and even if they could, there's none of it in the stores. Have you looked into our stores? (I had.) There's nothing on the shelves. There's not even beer, not even soda! Can you imagine that! Look, people need money, and the US has the money we need. That's what they really want – a comfortable life, a full stomach, and not to be bothered. What's the good of this *maldito* revolution if it just makes people hungry and unhappy? You think the people here like the Sandinistas? Not a bit. They're just afraid, their loyalty is skin-deep. They know what happens to them if they speak up. That's the way these communist *hijos de putas*, sons of whores, are. My own sister was killed by the Sandinistas. Yes, my sister. She spoke up and they took her and put her in jail and beat her. Then she died later on of kidney trouble, but it started then. The army is everything here, they take all the food from the people. Yes, that's where the food and everything good goes, and they kill you if you talk back. They have killed many Miskitu, don't believe otherwise, many Indians have been killed by these guys.

When Diego began I was too taken aback to reply. At first I thought that my shallow grasp of Spanish was mixing me up; but his meaning soon enough became unmistakable. Then I tried a few sensible ripostes, reminding him, for example, that the lack of beer might have something to do with the fact that the contras had blown up a bridge over which the beer was to be carried. But this was like spitting in the wind. And once Diego launched into his account of atrocities and human rights violations, I no longer had anything to say. What could appeal to his presumptive certainty? What was I going to say about the death of his sister? That he may be hysterical? My good impression of José González?

I had anticipated spending a good deal of time with Diego, but after fifteen minutes, I excused myself and retreated to my room. I had to be alone to sort this out. I was comfortable, thanks to my ant-proofing socks, and the room was lit. But if the evening before I had gone through physical darkness and bodily distress, this was to be my 'dark night of the soul'. It was not that Diego's words were any great surprise – after all, lots of people in Nicaragua, perhaps a third, dislike and even hate the Sandinistas, and many tell you so freely. Nor was I without the resources to construct a countervailing argument, for Diego was not very sophisticated, and very likely a victim of the vicious disinformation campaign hurled at Nicaragua, much of it beamed from Honduras by powerful radio transmitters, and probably heard by him on the very transistor radio he had purchased before the revolution. It is hard to exaggerate the lengths to which the US propaganda apparatus will go – I had learned, for example, of an instance where, in order to discredit a Sandinista vaccination campaign, the Indians were told that the vaccine had been prepared from Fidel Castro's urine, so that its use would infect children with communism! – and I could wax fairly eloquent on it and the related infamies practised by my government against the people of Nicaragua.

But there was nobody to debate with save myself. And nothing could gainsay certain unpleasant truths of the matter: first, I had no way of disproving Diego, for no degree of infamy or perfidy on one side could negate the possibility of infamy and perfidy on the other side. Appealing to numerous human rights investigations which never produced findings of the sort alleged by Diego might be suggestive, but it could not be conclusive. It would be supremely stupid to claim that one could begin to know all of what went on in even a very small country like Nicaragua. How could I disprove, for instance, that rather than going to sleep after my meeting with him, José González repaired instead to his special prison to torture Indians? Moreover, I would not even try to deny some of what Diego said, for example, about the gruesome economic situation. All I could do was shift the blame, or put the whole thing in 'perspective'. But whose perspective was I going to put it into? I, after all, didn't have to live through this mess. As thin as I was getting in Nicaragua, it would not be very long before my main dietary worry would be overeating. I was going to be able to complain all too soon about our materialistic consumer society. However much I shared the life of Nicaraguans, I remained at heart a tourist of the revolution.

This led to what was troubling me most of all – my own partiality, and the effects this may have been having on the soundness of my judgement. Viewed from the perspective of this little room in the house on stilts, the partiality began to smell of captivity.

I had no problem with the imperative to fight against the policy of my country in Central America, or to tackle the anticommunism that lies beneath that policy: such actions seemed adequately motivated by a sense of justice, even common sense. But I had gone further, having felt that it was not quite enough to be against; one also had to be for. Spurred on by feelings of sympathy, I had taken sides and become an advocate – had claimed not just that Reagan's policy was bad, but that the revolution was good. This put me into another position entirely from the vast majority of US citizens, even those who opposed Reagan in Central America. I have discovered that it is relatively easy to believe in revolution from anywhere in the world beyond the borders of the United States. Inside those borders, which needless to say can be transported in the mind to far-off Puerto Cabezas, an espousal of revolution is an assault on everything it means to be an 'American', for the United States is the counter-revolutionary society *par excellence*, the one place on earth today where all the forces opposing radical change mass themselves. For a United States citizen to actually like the Sandinistas is to run a gauntlet, all the more so if one is rash enough to think that other United States citizens should think better of the Nicaraguan revolution than they are supposed to. To be in this position is to be exposed to the nasty and recurring question: is one yet another dupe for 'communism', a fool who had not bothered to learn the lessons of the twentieth century? It doesn't take much to trigger this inquisition; Diego's diatribe had done the trick.

The nerve touched by Peter H was now aching as if from an inflamed tooth. Until now I had taken pride in my obscurity and immersion in the ordinary life of Nicaragua. Unlike some other observers from my homeland, I did not stay at the Hotel Intercontinental or come armed with letters from major US media sources assuring an Official Insider's view. This may have been making a virtue of necessity, but it was a virtue, nonetheless: largely on my own and struggling with day-to-day life in Nicaragua, it gave me a clearer, or at least a less cluttered perspective on what the revolution meant. Now I had broken this compact.

The tacit exchange with Freddy Balzan now appeared in a harsh light, and the light revealed a hitherto unexamined clause. Here, in Puerto Cabezas, I was the official guest of the revolution, rewarded to endorse it and spread its word. I was no longer a fly on the wall, observing quietly, but a beneficiary of the state and the Party. And he who pays the piper calls the tune. I had been paraded about by the Subcomandante himself, who was now my friend and who took me to his house, and announced me to an audience as an 'amigo de la humanidad' – surely more in the way of public praise than is my lot at home, where nothing comparable had happened since the American Legion awarded me the 'Most Likely to Succeed' medal at an assembly in High School. To be certified a friend to humanity is deeply appealing to narcissism. And nothing melts the critical faculties better than the glow of narcissistic satisfaction. Diego's diatribe had threatened the loss of that precious moment of authenticity, when I stood on the platform and felt at one with the great process of the revolution.

Suppose Diego were right?

Could I bear that? Suppose the people really just hated and feared the Sandinistas, and tolerated my friend González only so long as the army backed him up. Just because I loathed, say, Elliott Abrams, the Undersecretary of State in charge of crushing the Nicaraguan revolution, did this make Abrams wrong? Of course, one could punch holes in the arguments of Abrams, or Ronald Reagan, or whoever was on 'their' side. Why, however, should I exempt the arguments of my side, especially when there is so much desire to be right? The deep, intractable misery of Nicaragua swam before me: the kitchen-worker shuddering with fear on the cot in the Hospital Siquiátrico; the patient, wraith-like people breathing in the fumes on the Pista de la Resistencia while they waited forever for their bus; Pavel's mother wandering the streets; the malarial children staring from their hospital beds; the little girl who saw her two brothers fall to the contras; the hunger, hunger, hunger and the 'no hay' . . . Yes it was Reagan's fault; but no, it was not only Reagan, and not only his henchmen either. They were reacting to something, playing a role in a larger scheme in which the other side – my side – was playing its role, too. We all were responsible. Why couldn't we leave things alone?

Was I romanticizing revolution, polishing up or simply denying its flaws, compensating for the flaws and frustrations of my own life by promoting the rebellion of these desperate people against the great Father Figure in Washington, helping to push them into misery for the sake of an abstract ideal? How much bloodshed had been inflicted upon the world by intellectuals who lead the suffering masses to revolt instead of simply giving them bread? Well, yes, the revolt came from below, and no revolution could ever be imported, and so forth, as I had said many times. But this truth could also be a self-serving over-simplification. Old Lenin, whom many of us would like to forget, pointed out the necessity for a 'vanguard' of leadership – read, intellectuals – to give shape to the unconscious revolutionary longings of the masses, and history was not about to disprove him.

My friend Diego now began to seem like Dostoevsky's Grand Inquisitor. The people don't want this so-called 'freedom', ran an inner voice. It was a well-oiled voice, carefully implanted over the years, and I hated it. But my hatred didn't make the voice wrong, especially as it called itself the voice of reason. Give them bread, security, not the torment of revolution, went the voice. Yes, capitalism has plundered them; but that is past, a time of primitive excesses. Nobody is perfect; and only capitalism has shown the ability to adapt. Now it offers the best chance of a rational development to bring bread to all, and security from revolutionary madness, from marxism, from communism. You can bet that as soon as the marines take Puerto Cabezas, the shelves are going to fill with bread and meat, television sets, and of course, plenty of beer and soda.

THE TESTAMENT

After about an hour of this misery, something of an answer to my dilemma occurred to me. I scribbled it in my notebook, and would like to reproduce it here – or rather, expand it and truncate it a bit: expand its substance, and cut out out its preliminaries. You have heard all the preliminaries before; or if not, you can find them scattered throughout the numberless works which obsessively watch the Nicaraguan revolution and tell us sombrely of its many flaws and its many achievements, adding them all up in columns, and asking the reader to decide if the Sandinistas deserve a stay of execution or not. And so I will not detail all the bad things about the revolution which Diego's diatribe suggested: the backwardness of the nation in which it occurs, its disastrous economy, the difficult problem posed by a strong party such as the FSLN which can identify itself with the state, pretty well control the flow of information and squeeze out opposition, and the challenge to democratic process this entails. Neither will I attempt to defend the revolution from the charges of a world which holds it perpetually in the dock (though I probably will not be able to resist the temptation from time to time), nor thread my way through the labyrinth of the highly politicized question of human rights. And finally, I am not going to detail all the good things the revolution has done: the redistribution of land, the literacy campaign, the advances in health care, all carried out in the teeth of a violent counter-revolution led by the United States.

The economic disaster in which Nicaragua finds itself, the indubitable fact that years of turmoil have worsened the overall material level, the brutal suffering the people are going through as a result – all of this is excruciatingly painful to anyone who cares about the country. But the condition of Nicaragua is not due to some revolutionary or 'communist' structure which hits the nation like a meteorite from outer space. It is rather due to an ever-developing process in which revolutionary and counter-revolutionary elements are both always active and vying with each other. So long as events remain in the context of the imperialism and counter-revolution which always accompany a revolution, we cannot form any singular judgement, nor crudely blame, like a Diego. If we remember that in the years before Reagan launched his war to prove that 'communism' doesn't work, the economy of revolutionary Nicaragua was growing by 8 to 10 percent per annum, and even exporting food to that model of capitalist development, Costa Rica, we should not be too facile in dismissing the practical capacities of the Sandinistas. And if we bear in mind that nearby Cuba, having endured counter-revolution, has been able to bring the standard of living of the people to paradisaical levels by the standards of the Latin American poor, we are not

143

entitled to reject the possibilities of socialism in a country like Nicaragua (which in any event has opted for a mixed model of development). The real question is, in which direction should we go? And the answer to this has to take into account more than economic practicality, or hewing to established political values. It has to include these, to be sure, but in a framework of values which have not yet been established – the full, realized needs of human beings.

I don't want to talk therefore about 'things' at all, but about the 'spirit' of the revolution. Because it seems to me that this is what the commentators miss but the participants live and die for. And it was why I came to Nicaragua – and why thousands of other people have come to Nicaragua – and it represents what the revolution is finally worth, after all, whatever Diego, or Ronald Reagan, or Elliott Abrams say about the Sandinistas. But of course I don't think what they say is true, either. Anyhow, what I wrote went something like this. I'm not sure whether or not it answers the nagging inner voice set going by Diego. I'm not sure there is an answer anyhow. You be the judge.

After everything has been said about a revolution, after all the pundits, scholars, critics, commentators, commissioners, Congressional committees, journalists, jurists, historians, anthropologists, political scientists, sociologists, novelists, film-makers, documentarians and just plain tourists have gathered their notes, taken their snapshots, filed their reports, published their tomes and gone home . . . after all this, the revolution remains. It is, finally, irreducibly, there. Revolution is an event, or process, that cannot be enclosed in any fence of abstract and logical statements, cannot be tied up in any neat package. I am not trying to be mystical, or to deny the possibility of saying very important, useful and true things about revolutions. Nor am I trying to say that we have to be agnostic about revolution because, like God, it can never be known. No, just the opposite: we have to know everything we can about revolutions – far, far more than I can tell you in this fragment of my life in Nicaragua – and we have consciously to judge the value of a revolution and decide where we stand with respect to it. Consciously, say, because we fall into line, one way or the other, unconsciously if not consciously; indeed, there can be no agnosticism when a revolution challenges the global centre of power.

But I must say this: after everything is said and weighed and added up and balanced, revolutions do not make sense. Too much is upset, too much is confused, too much of the old order remains amidst the new. Including, of course, the old order of our thinking. And yet we must decide.

To judge a process that makes so many demands upon us, that puts so much in a new light, that divides families against each other and divides individuals within themselves and throws people outside themselves, that stirs up violence from the bottom of the pot and puts men and women to the test as nothing else in the world, to decide, in other words, where we stand, we need more than the sum total of objective knowledge about revolution. We need to begin with that knowledge, we cannot do without that knowledge, but all the objective knowledge in the world will not answer the single insistent question a revolution poses: the question of our engagement with it. Where do we stand? That is a question which has to be answered at the level of the spirit, subjectively and existentially. And it cannot be legislated or delegated. Each person must decide in the stillness of his or her soul. A revolution redistributes the wealth of a nation and it creates new human possibilities. Both of these levels are essential, and connected with each other. But at heart they are very different; for one has to do with the distribution of things, the other with the creation of spirit. It is at this latter level that the question of engagement is posed. What is the quality of the spirit of a revolution? This is not something to be decided too quickly – and it can never be decided at a distance or through abstractions: civil liberties, Marxism-Leninism, imperialism. It has to be decided on the ground, by living a revolution, by experiencing its disordered, tattered and crazy soul – or at the least, by feeling it in one's own soul.

Ah, you may say, here comes the 'soul' of the revolution; perhaps the same soul Hitler invoked, the mystical union of the German people with 'blood'. Or is it to be the glorious soul of the Iranians summoned by Khomeini, or of the Cambodians by Pol Pot, the soul of Apartheid, or Zionism, or the Tamils, or the IRA? Even Reagan's appeal to the soul of the US? So many Souls! Each embodied in a nationalist aspiration, bringing a people out of bondage and into history. Each reducing all others, all who stand in the way of the glorious project of destiny, to the role of Other, the stranger who can be eliminated for the sake of the higher synthesis. We must not fool ourselves: once the soul or spirit is invoked, the way has been cleared for intolerance and fanaticism, the forging of a social body as an instrument to crush all before it. In fact, the intolerant, fanatical national spirit bears an exact resemblance to the image of the Sandinist revolution that Diego, Elliott Abrams and Ronald Reagan would have us believe. After all, that is what a totalitarian repressive police state is like. Whether or not we think that the real flesh-and-blood Sandinistas are in fact like that, we should take the charge seriously. No matter how often we can prove Reagan a liar or his client-states the real villains, we should still recognize that every revolutionary project has the seeds of intolerance and repression in it – and the more radical and thoroughgoing the revolution, the more seeds does it have.

Perhaps we should stay out of this domain entirely, and cite the advancement in health care, or the proof that the elections of 1984 were democratic, or that charges of human rights violations against the Sandinistas have been trumped up. Perhaps these objective things are true and it would be safer to stay with them. But it would also be pointless. Because what we call soul is the real gateway to what defines us as human in this world. It can open upon evil, and it can open upon good. But if it is not opened, then we go nowhere at all. In any case, nothing has been settled by talking at such a level. We are back with abstractions – of 'soul' or 'spirit' now, in place of human rights or imperialism. And there is no one homogeneous world-soul or spirit. There are only particular, historically shaped souls and spirits. The question is not whether spirit has been crucial in the Nicaraguan revolution, because it is crucial in all revolutions. Nor is it whether the revolution can be wished away, for it has been thrust upon us by an unravelling of a history of imperial domination, which has been going on all over the world simply because it has been built into the structure of our societies. The question is rather, what is the quality of the spirit of this revolution? This one crazy and improbable revolution. What is the concrete, material nature of its spirit? Is the spirit of Nicaragua as

Reagan and the rest tell us, or is there something else to it which takes it away from the path traced by the intolerant and fanatical revolutionary movements and towards a real universalism?

This is a crucial question, so far as I am concerned, even if it cannot be settled objectively. Let me repeat: it is not the only essential question. There is no point in talking of the soul of a revolution unless the revolution also sincerely moves toward redistributing the goods of the earth. We talk a lot about human rights, but there is no human right which supersedes the right of people to see that their children do not starve, the right of everybody to an equal share of the health resources of a society, and so forth. (In this light, how 'democratic' is the United States?) If I do not emphasize these things here, it is because others have done so elsewhere, while there is something else which has perhaps been spoken of less. And that has to do with the concrete quality of the Nicaraguan spirit. But how is this to be talked of, if it can never be pinned down objectively?

Let me have a go at it. Before a people become conscious of themselves and in charge of their destiny, they must stop being the way they were. It is in this transition that the experiential dynamic of revolution lies. A good way of describing the change which revolution opens up for individual lives is that of giving oneself to it, and to the people one shares it with. This is how we stop being who we were and start being somebody else, for better or worse. If revolutionary giving goes well, it can lead to nonviolence and emancipation. If it goes badly, it leads to a loss of the self in the totalitarian system and a reinstitutionalization of violence.

'Give' was the word used by a doctor in Chontales (a region where the counter-revolution is strongly entrenched) on one of my earlier visits to Nicaragua. He was a man of the upper classes, expatriated by the dictatorship, who gave up a lucrative and comfortable professional life in Canada to return and work under the most frightful, impecunious and arduous conditions for the revolution. He struck me as a radiantly happy person. 'La esencia del Sandinismo es dar', he had said at the conclusion of a talk outlining his work, and the word *dar* – to give – had stuck with me, less because I understood its specific reference to the revolution, than because its opposite – to take – seemed the most apt way of

147

putting into one word what the *ancien régime* was all about. One doesn't like to oversimplify, but the pairing, give–take, had a feel about it which suggested it was close to the heart of revolution. In any case, I had been thinking about it since.

The self we surrender in a revolution is a precipitate of the past; and when we give it up we surrender the past and potentially renew ourselves. For the ex-objects of history, the Nicaraguans, the self to be given up is the seat of passivity and fatalism: the humiliated self that inertly accepted the mind of the master. And for the *internacionalista* from the First World, the self to be given up is the prideful self, the all-possessing, ethnocentric White man's Ego. These are the necessary first steps of a revolutionary change; the rest of the way remains to be chosen, for better or worse.

Let me put these reflections down on the ground. We ultimately play our historical parts for many unseen reasons, but these unseen reasons are refracted through concrete experience – and real human beings. In other words, the immediate cause of our political action is some personal relationship. Lying there in the guest house, thinking about the revolution as a whole, I did not see the revolution as a whole, I only saw the figures through whom the revolution was refracted. I saw Freddy Balzan, and thought of the shrimp I owed him; and I saw José González, and thought of the danger he is subjected to, and his adolescence given to the mountains; and I thought of Pedro Joaquín Romero and his dignity, and Rita Arauz and Doña Clara from the mountains, and a host of others. And I thought of Diego, sitting stolidly in the next room, and maybe Mr Bragman, too, and Elliott Abrams plotting away in Washington.

And I realized that I had been getting it all wrong. Not in detail, but in framework, in basic conception. I had thought – how could I think otherwise, given where I came from? – in terms of an exchange with Freddy, José and the revolution: they give me this, I give them that back, in return. It would be a deal. But this conception of giving was utterly outside what the revolution really meant. It was rather exactly what the revolution was there to transcend: the market relations of the *ancien régime*. These latter were ego-giving, in which each party remained intact in the fortress of the self, while he gave detachable property to get something back

of equal or greater value. In other words, its giving was subordin-
ated to possessing. It was precisely this exchange-giving which
maintained the status quo that had denied humanity to the bulk of
the world's people. Such a state of affairs cannot be equably
rectified, because it is rooted in deep existential attitudes as much as
in material things. There is no way, therefore, a revolution can even
out the status quo. If it succeeds, even without institutionalizing
violence, the old power structure is injured, and many people who
have had the goods of society suffer and leave the country; while
even those who come out on top suffer greatly in one way or
another. If, on the other hand, the revolution fails, the new life is
snuffed out – for a time. In any case, something must give, and
individuals must choose.

Our power structure, perhaps all existing power, is one of
possessiveness. Possessing – taking and exchanging – is what built
our world, with its prodigious wealth and its atomistic, fragmented
human beings. Possessing is what ordinary economic activity is
about. It generates the detachable things called commodities; and it
leads to the paranoid hostility of the Hobbesian jungle where each
is against all, which is what we charitably call 'free enterprise'. The
realm of exchange produces a kind of egoistical pride, which marks
those formed by the First World: the pride, for instance, which
flared in me with José González's praise in the auditorium before
the Miskitus. It also produces a characteristic liberal political type –
a kind of individual who proclaims a notion of freedom based on
separate individuals, but fails to notice that this 'freedom' is a
condition for the predatory expansion of the First World at the
expense of the Third World. These self-styled 'democrats' came
down to Nicaragua to massage their self-esteem by scolding the
Sandinistas, telling them, in effect, 'Why can't you be more like us?
Rejoin our superior, white civilization defined by the Monroe
Doctrine and the Big Stick'. Some of these people will oppose
Ronald Reagan. They may even donate material aid to Nicaragua.
What they cannot relinquish is their sense of superiority.

If the revolution means anything – to whoever participates in it –
it means a radical decentring in which the notion of exchange
simply breaks down. What was I going to do, with my pen – my
'arma' or weapon as José had called it – my pen and my itching

149

ankles, to repay González and Balzan? For what? For spending one's youth being eaten alive under the mountain rains, one's manhood facing assassination or eventual destruction at the hands of a violent superpower – my superpower? What was the equation here? Why, there was none, there was no equivalence at all . . . which meant that one either pulled back into fortress-America, fortress-ego; or opened up, and gave, going onward into a zone of non-predictability and renewal.

There may have been no equivalence at the level of object, of what I could *do*; but there is another equivalence opened onto by the revolution, and that is equivalence at the level of subject, of who I *am*, of who we *are*. There is no exchanging being, but once one has given, there is sharing it, participating in it, experiencing it as mutuality, at the level of *compañero*. This is what revolution offers instead of exchange. Its great, singular, non-egoic gift: all men and women are brothers and sisters. No doubt an easily mouthed slogan – yet lived when one gives one's self to the revolution. It is the one distinct superiority of the revolution over the counter-revolution, and the reason beyond all others why there is no dignity to the counter-revolution and why its project can never be ennobling, but must lead to barbarity. And it was why the revolution produced so much joy, because it undid the fatal discontinuity of being which all humans abhor. It was a mixture of this genuine exaltation, this transcendence, along with my old-style narcissism, or pride, that I felt on the platform at the 'Acto' with González. And it was the conflict set into motion between those two states of being that I was playing out after my conversation with Diego, for the latter's words had sharpened the contradiction between the two states and made them irreconcilable. Diego forced me to choose, or rather, to continue choosing, for which I thank him.

As for Diego, whatever the merits of what he said, it was clear that he remained outside of what the revolution was trying to do. His practical, common-sensical view spoke to the stomach, and perhaps even a narrow portion of the head; but it left out the heart and soul, and froze him in time. He had chosen – how consciously is not at issue – to remain an object of the *ancien régime*, dreaming of the day when the white overlord, perhaps Mr Bragman himself, would return and shower Puerto Cabezas with his rain of commodities. Diego, in sum, gave nothing of himself. There were others with the counter-revolution of whom it can be said that they give of themselves, and perhaps believe as sincerely as José González in what they are doing. I would suspect that the unlucky Colonel Oliver North is of this kind; which is what makes him such a hero to the right wing. But there is an essential difference between giving oneself to the oppressor and to the oppressed. The first pathway closes in toward a fascist spirit, because it is giving in the interests of taking. It is giving to those who have robbed and expropriated, and it can only lead to destruction. How can people be true brothers and sisters when the jealous Father remains in command? The second pathway, by contrast, is giving to those who have already given, to those who have been robbed. It is a pathway which opens outward, toward the universality of human beings, the realization of our species.

This is spirituality of a different kind, and a politics of a different kind. We might call it being a 'spiritual warrior'. Of course, the people – internationalists and native Nicaraguans alike – I knew in Nicaragua who lived this way didn't think in such terms, which smack so much of the self-indulgent New Age culture. If pressed, most would just say, as did a physician-friend who gave up many comforts to work in Nicaragua, that 'things just make more sense here', or words to that effect. But although we may dislike the jargon of spirituality, the reality behind that jargon, that there is in human beings a drive for breaking through the barriers of the given, continues insistently in many lives. And for such spirits, a revolution like Nicaragua's provides a matchless opportunity to express that drive in a materially significant way.

It is a calling, much like the original political impulses of the Puritans. And a giving, too: the hope of giving one's life over to a quest of selflessness. One might say that revolution opens up the possibility of a sincere existence; not just belief, but one's whole being becomes integral. Although the quest, like all human desires, is bound to fall short of fulfilment, to have lived this way, even in a fleeting moment, is precious. And to have had the opportunity to live this way for the poor – and not, as a protofascist like Oliver North, for the exploiters – is a gift to amply repay any hardship.

151

Having arrived at this point, my reflections could return to the question of the FSLN in power. It now seemed to me that the party belonged to the zone of necessity, and that it played the same role toward the revolution as a parent did toward a newborn child. A revolution is far more than the government of its society; but it needs that government, and the revolutionary party has to understand, express and meet that need. From another angle, the party has to mediate between the astonishing presence of this newborn particle of transcendence, and the historically made world which both needs this renewal and would destroy it. The party is the guardian of the revolution; it is not the revolution itself. The party's job is to see that the revolution survives, and then to efface itself. Can the party succeed? Well, don't bet on it. After all, the party has to conform to the old world if it is going to survive and help the revolution survive. It cannot simply negate the old order of things, since it has been shaped by it, must live within it, make war against it, do all sorts of things which are far removed from the pure centre of revolutionary transcendence. And power corrupts, and revolutionary ardour cannot be eaten, and so forth. There is no reason, therefore, why a party, like anybody else in power, cannot revert to the pattern of taking and lose themselves in domination.

Given all that stands in its way, it is safe to predict that the FSLN will probably fail in the long run. It will not bring the perfect human order into being. Now this realization might produce consternation in some quarters. But it doesn't bother most of the people I know in Nicaragua who give of themselves for the revolution, knowing full well, with a clear mind not at all blinded by enthusiasm, that the Sandinistas are only fallible human beings facing superhuman odds, and that there is no way Nicaragua would ever approach perfection. But who ever said we had to have the millennium, or utopia? Is the revolution supposed to substitute for God? Is it not enough to have brought this new life into the world and nourished it for a while? To have fought the good fight, helped a people ennoble themselves, given them a real history instead of ignominy? And passed the torch on. In fact, almost everybody I knew who worked for the revolution was simply grateful and amazed that it had lasted as long as it has, that Reagan's troops were not in the streets of Managua by mid-1987, that so much had been done, and so many lessons learned, that such a storehouse of revolutionary lore had been gathered to be shared with those who are to come later. For a revolution is a precious achievement of human culture.

Ah, but the Sandinista revolution is Marxist, too, goes the standard complaint, meaning, in the context of the way we talk of these things, that it has suffered the kiss of death. Now one is supposed to be ashamed of this Marxism in our society, where anticommunism rains down on us every day. At this point in the argument one is supposed to say, well, I'm sorry, you know, but they aren't really Marxists, or they aren't the bad kind of Marxists, or they won't let the Soviets in . . . whatever it takes to mollify the touchy feelings of the Northamericans, to reassure them that their continent won't be taken away from them. But this gets at the whole thing in the wrong way, does it not? Because, yes, even though they have been careful to retain a mixed economy, the Sandinistas are Marxists, and even to some degree, Marxist-Leninist. And no, there is no reason to be ashamed of this or explain it away. Because they are Marxists for the very sensible reason that one does not define oneself in opposition to the power of the Yankee and become a historical subject unless one assumes the position of the philosophy of revolution. And Marxism happens to be the philosophy of revolution wherever revolution occurs in a land controlled by capitalism; whilst Leninism, that is, the development of a strong party as the controlling force of the revolution, happens to be the only historical means for revolutions to survive in the face of the inevitable counter-revolution. If there were no counter-revolution, there would be no need for a strong party. This would be nice, but it is an utter fantasy. The last time a socialist revolution tried to come into being by parliamentary democratic means was in Chile in the days of Salvador Allende – and it may very well have been the last such instance. The lessons of Chile were not lost on the Sandinistas, who did not need to be reminded, in any event, of the savagery of the dictatorship and the global order behind it. It may be added, though this is not the place to pursue the point, that what is taking place in Nicaragua amounts to a genuine mutation of Marxism-Leninism under the influence of native traditions, radical Christianity, and other tendencies. Therefore when a member of the

153

ruling group says that s/he is a 'Sandinist', and not a 'Marxist', s/he is not being evasive. In any case, I see no need to apologize for these revolutionaries.

It seems deeply wrong to feel sorry for the Nicaraguan people, or deplore what Washington is doing to Nicaragua, and then 'balance' this with the ritualistic attack upon the Sandinistas, as if they were in some measure 'unworthy' of the people, or betrayers of their ideals. If you take the side of the Nicaraguan people, in their dignity, joy and martyrdom, as against feeling sorry for them, then you take the side of those who dedicate their lives to the revolution. Taking their side doesn't mean holding back from criticism. It means criticizing as someone who feels for the revolution. There is no contradiction between revolution and the critical faculties. On the contrary, becoming a historical subject means an expansion of mind. In fact, many Nicaraguans become brilliant through their revolutionary struggle.

In any case, the Sandinistas have not been unworthy of the revolution, and Nicaragua, for all its flaws, has not gone the way of domination. They have made their mistakes, but they have not fallen into the abyss, have not cut themselves off from their people, and have shown themselves capable of learning and adapting. Being human and in the awful spot they are in, they remain capable of destroying what they have built and of institutionalizing violence. This could happen any time, but it did not happen, so far as I know, during my time in Nicaragua, nor while I was writing this. Their genius may be the result of consciously learning the lessons of previous revolutions, or it may be a historical accident. For there is a generosity of soul to the Nicaraguan, which is reflected in the revolution they make. The Sandinistas do not have to be taught to give. They may simply be virtuosi of revolution.

There is another way of saying this, impossible to avoid in a nation so deeply imbued with religion. The Nicaraguans – and the Sandinistas, Marxist or no – are people of the spirit. That is the 'quality of their spirit' – to be spiritual. There are mean-spirited people, fanatical and intolerant-spirited people . . . and there are spiritual people. The Nicaraguans have all types, but the latter is characteristic. How do we talk about this? I don't really know. I can only point to what I saw in Nicaragua, to the astounding intensity of existence there, and hope that you will see for yourself. Let me say clumsily though, that as low as Nicaragua falls materially, so high does it become raised up in the spirit. And I think, too, that the spiritual quality of the Nicaraguan revolution, which is but another side of its generosity, is what has saved it from disaster. If the Sandinistas have not rigidified their revolution and made it an end in itself, it is because they have retained a sense of the spirit – of something beyond, something not encompassed in political power.

I had seen this at first hand in so many people, had felt it pull at my own soul so many times. I am sure it is the force that brought me to Nicaragua. The image of Gabriel Bell comes again to mind as I write this, the face transfigured, no doubt an ordinary man, who gave of himself into a spiritual greatness I had believed required the genius of the Italian Renaissance to depict. But Bell, and so many like him, had become geniuses of their own. And he was a martyr. I recall the words of Indiana Acevedo, another genius, a woman of the People's Church who lived in San Judas, one of Managua's poorest barrios, where she counselled the mothers of soldiers. As Indiana said to me one day:

> La sangre de los que han muerto lo vemos en los platos cuando comemos, lo vemos en las calles cuando caminamos . . . lo más valioso que nosotros tenemos en este pueblo es la sangre de los mártires; éllos no permiten que nosotros vacilemos.*

The martyr is the person who has given the most, has borne the most witness. To paraphrase Che Guevara, at the risk of seeming ridiculous, the revolution, its pure flame, is contained in this spirituality. No individual citation can convey the reality of what I mean, because the reality is in the web between people. This pattern between the people sharing this moment of crisis is the new historical subject, in the agony, pain and joy of its birth. Here a truly startling meaning adheres to Nicaragua. This wretchedly poor nation, condemned as 'Marxist-Leninist', despised by the fashion-

---

* We see the blood of those who have died on our plates when we eat; we see it in the streets when we walk. The greatest value this people holds is the blood of its martyrs. They will not permit us to vacillate.

able centres of the world and bled dry by the superpower, is to many of its own people – and to people elsewhere, too – nothing else than a contemporary incarnation of Jesus on the Cross. The searing contrast between the spiritual level of people one sees in Nicaragua and the power structure – let us say it: the Herods and Pontius Pilates – of the Reagan administration brings the myth to life.

Look at the martyred Gabriel Bell. Look at Elliott Abrams. Then decide for yourself. The revolution is more, finally, than the sum of the revolutionaries, who are only its guardians. It is a mode of being that happens to people and brings them out of their previous selves, gives them a way of transcendence. It is a rupture, a singularity that undoes an existing situation of historical repression and releases spiritual energy. And so it spreads and belongs to the world. After all, the world, and especially the United States, made Nicaragua the way it is. Now Nicaragua changes everything else. Direct revolutionary transformation is no longer an issue in the industrialized nations. This only means, however, that our social control mechanisms are too well implanted for radical change. It says nothing about whether we need radical change – whether this society built on possessiveness has abandoned the soul in its search for power, and whether people feel this as a curse, or whether we need to be emancipated from this burden ... or whether the spiritual force of the Nicaraguan revolution has the potential to emancipate us from ourselves.

Words such as Indiana Acevedo's are not going to be spoken in the Upper West Side of Manhattan, or in San Diego, where this is being written. That is out of the question. The question is, can they be heard here? I think many of us can hear, recognize and respond to them. Many of us know that we have become imprisoned in ourselves. As we have become attached to objects, so have we become objects, objects to the petrified idol of the self, objects of our own narcissism, our whiteness. I think that many of us want to change this condition radically, even if we are shocked to associate the change we want with the concept of a Marxist revolution. The Nicaraguan revolution can help free us from the prison-house of the self. Of course, not passively, but only as we affirm it, immerse ourselves in it, identify with it and become

156

historical subjects through critical participation in its struggle. Or to put this all in one sentence: to the extent we give of ourselves to it. Just as we participated in the immiseration of the nations of the Third World so are we capable of being transformed by their transformation. Once we sent missionaries to the colonies. Now, this revolution sends a mission to us.

I would not say this had I not seen it happen in literally dozens of instances. I have seen, that is, people from North and South becoming better than they were, more expansive, more dedicated, more clear-headed, more committed, focused and hopeful – in sum, more universal – by giving themselves to the Nicaraguan revolution. And my experience has been multiplied manyfold. Tens of thousands have responded to Nicaragua, from the United States and throughout the world. They have given, in all the ways that human beings can give. When the contras kidnapped a construction brigade from West Germany during my visit, a call for replacements produced volunteers from twenty-one different countries within one day. When the United States came within a hair of invading in November 1983, a million Mexicans were said to volunteer to fight for Nicaragua. And in Vermont today, the City of Burlington declares Puerto Cabezas its sister, and holds a festival whose proclamation is 'Vermont is Nicaragua'. Even the Upper West Side of Manhattan has adopted a sister city, the tiny town of Santa Bárbara.

Vilified, bled dry, the nation on the Cross radiates the bonding power of the revolutionary spirit. No wonder the Reagan administration wants to crush Nicaragua.

GOODBYE TO PUERTO CABEZAS

After I had written the notes upon which this testament is based, I slept well; and the next day, Monday, passed smoothly and busily. Yvonne had the whole day at my disposal, Fernando had a better vehicle, and I had a list of destinations and people to see. We tooled about town, noting the new Cuban-aided housing development on the outskirts, and the new hospital under construction by a brigade of militia. We visited the old hospital, with its cases of malaria and unpacked crates of sterilizers, X-ray machinery and water distillers donated by the people of sister Burlington. When the new facility opened, these would be used. Meanwhile, surgery had come to a halt for lack of oxygen, and the vintage 1949 X-ray equipment worked scarcely at all (which might not be such an entirely bad thing, considering the radiation it emitted when it did). This was the only place in Nicaragua, I was told, where starving children with swollen bellies were seen. The poorest people in the whole country were the Indians from the interior. Ex-miners, they now faced starvation until the mines could be reopened. And this was impossible thanks to Mr Reagan.

I also learned that Freddy Balzan would not get his shrimp. Once the major cash crop of the region, there was now a 'no hay camarones' situation because of the war and the awful state of the jetty. Another triumph for the intrepid Reagan.

In the afternoon we visited Hazel Lau, a tiny and fiery woman who is the elected Representative of the Miskitu to the National Assembly. Hazel was one of the founders of Misurasata, the principal indigenous rights group. Later she broke with Brooklyn Rivera, at present a main opposition leader, and cast in her lot with the Sandinistas. Now she spends half her time in Managua and half here, in the ramshackle regional office for the Indians, where she holds court to the people who travel for days from remote areas of the province to voice their needs. Hazel is very sanguine. The prospect of the 100 million dollars which had just been allocated by Congress worried her not a bit. The money, according to Hazel, was a 'círculo vicioso' for the counter-revolution, which only stimulated their greed, alienated them from the people, and cost them far more in political support than they ever would gain militarily. There was a time when the armed Miskitu resistance could pretend to represent the desires of the Indians, as a kind of third force between the revolution and imperialism. Now there could be no question that they were part of imperialism, and the people would see that there had been only two choices all along.

There was one more name on my list, another Miskitu named César Pais, who was Vice Chairman of the Autonomy Commission. Yvonne was unable to arrange a meeting during the day but said he would see me that night. Accordingly, after an evening spent visiting various citizens of Puerto Cabezas, we strolled over to the barracks of the Ministry of the Interior, knocked at the gate and asked for Compañero Pais. It was 11.00 p.m. At length a short and heavy-set young man came out. I could not place where I had seen him before, although he recognized me right away. 'Don't you remember, Saturday morning? I took you into town.' He had been the officer who had picked me up, sopping wet, in his blue jeep, inspected my papers and, I am sure, watched over me ever since. He was no longer dour, though, but affable, even jovial. But then, I was no longer a dripping stranger of obscure origin, but a certifiable friend of the revolution.

César suggested that we speak in his offices in the compound, and I agreed, pleased at the thought of another inside look at Sandinista power. But the door to the office was jammed. No other offices being open, we repaired to my quarters, where we were greeted by Diego. I did not know whether to be alarmed. Should I inform César that the Mestizo sitting absently on the other side of the room was no friend of the Sandinistas? Lurid spy fantasies crept into my thoughts, but I held my peace. The idea of informing on Diego was absurd. Anyway, what state secrets was César Pais going to tell me?

As it turned out, if Diego was an informer to the counter-revolution, then all he was going to be able to tell his superiors was that the Sandinistas are awfully confident of the situation. César Pais was if possible more sanguine than Hazel Lau and José González. Perhaps it was because of an agreement which had been hammered out that day at Yulu, a hamlet 35 kilometres to the north-east of Puerto Cabezas. César proudly read through the terms of the peace accord between the government and the dissident Miskitu faction of that region. One more brick in the edifice. He went on to recount the other signs of triumph: 70 percent of the troops now guarding Northern Zelaya are from the region itself. Miskitus are playing an ever-increasing role in the local government. Only three years ago, there was no direct contact between the Sandinistas and the Indians. Now, no more inter-mediaries were needed. When the two sides talked, they talked face to face 'a pesar de la agresión'. In spite of the aggression.

The next morning the wind was up and the rain heavier than usual. Worse yet, Yvonne was late. A moment of panic. Was this

159

the 'tormenta' that Freddy had warned me against? Was I going to have to spend the rest of the week in Puerto Cabezas? Was I going to spend the rest of my life here, listening to the shutters creaking and the rain drumming against the roof? I suddenly realized how badly I wanted to get out of Puerto Cabezas.

And then Yvonne pulled up, and later, the FAS plane came in from Managua, just on time, swooping through the sodden sky and onto the lonely airstrip. I was properly booked and only had to await the unloading of the cargo before boarding. I recalled the load of coffins which had accompanied the Saturday flight. What strategic freight would the plane be bringing this time for the besieged and embattled town? The bay doors opened and the young men in olive-green began unloading several stacks of boxes. As I entered the plane, I recognized the familiar red, white and blue label on the bottles. The Pepsi Cola had arrived. Pepsi Cola for Puerto Cabezas.

6

THE
GIFT

THURSDAY MORNING in front of the US Embassy was the
high point of the week. I tried to be one of the first to arrive,
sometimes even getting there before Jim and Margaret Goff
set up their spindly microphone and amplifier. Mary Hartman
might be there, too, more gaunt, if that is possible, than Jim Goff.
Toughened by years and years of the tropical sun, the Catholic nun
and the Presbyterian minister had each given themselves over to the
revolution. But if Mary was sustained by an unquenchable
optimism, Jim appeared to live on outrage. He seemed to me
perpetually aghast, blinking with fury at the calumnies committed
by the US against his beloved Nicaragua. Jim devised broadsides
against the latest pack of right-wing lies from his cluttered office at
the Centro Antonio Valdivieso, headquarters of the liberation
church, while Margaret, who served as archivist, painstakingly
clipped stories and maintained the files down the hall. Mary
Hartman's bailiwick was the Human Rights Commission – the one
which liked the government of Nicaragua, that is, there being
another Commission more or less in league with the counter-
revolution. Though they seemed to be looking at the revolution
from opposite points of the compass, the names and locations of
the two commissions were confusingly close.

On my first trip, I went to a meeting of the Committee of US
Citizens Living In Nicaragua. Asking the way to the 'Comisión

de los derechos humanos', where I had been told the meeting was to be held, I was directed down a maze of streets to a modest two-storey building. It had the name, 'Derechos Humanos', all right, but there were no gringos, nor any trappings of the revolution on the walls. I was greeted instead with countless images of the Holy Father, Pope John Paul II, and his lieutenant, Miguel Obando y Bravo, the Archbishop of Managua. There was no need to ask whether this was a wrong number.

The pro-Sandinista group of US citizens were certainly an odd lot, bound together by love for Nicaragua and a sense of monstrous and continuing unfairness. This was not only because of terrorism against the Nicaraguan people; it also reflected the mental atrocities committed in the battle for the minds of fellow citizens: the propagation of an enemy psychosis, the disinformation, the double standards, the whole apparatus of anticommunism. Indeed, we lived in sustained indignation. We knew how badly the people back home are hoodwinked about Nicaragua, and how the lies open the gate for the war which has already cost Nicaragua more per capita than World War Two did the United States. These feelings burn and choke inside, all the more so because the war was a 'low intensity' operation, such being the name devised by the security apparatus to do Vietnam-type operations without the political cost of Vietnam. The low-intensity war is a real war, and except for the detail of using mercenaries instead of Northamerican boys, a total war. However, because of the political strategy , it is also a long, protracted torment carried out with civility and diplomatic relations. According to the rules of the game, Nicaragua has to take it on the chin while smiling and remaining the model of decorum. Any breach of politeness, and the hounds of world opinion would start baying, thus permitting Uncle Sam to get in a few more gouges, or even to go all the way for the kill.

We got our satisfaction, however, in front of the fortress-embassy every Thursday morning at 7.30. It is a time of day when Managua seems habitable, a time when all the gringos in Nicaragua can gather against the Yankee and a person can sustain for at least one half-hour the illusion that the majority of Americans are politically progressive. In Managua this might just be true. Maybe. I'm not sure, because I don't know exactly how many US citizens are living permanently or semi-permanently in Managua, or how many troop through, in delegations of teachers, Lutherans, nuns, or nurses from Des Moines, St Louis, Portland or Phoenix, to pay their respects to the land of Sandino and bear witness to the aggression made by their government.

Nor did we know for sure how many Yankees are stationed at the Embassy, or how many marines are there to guard them, or how many of the mysterious-looking cars, some of recent US vintage, contain members of the shadowy business community or spooks from the CIA, or how many old hangers-on from the days when Managua was a Yankee pleasure dome, or how many visiting Congressmen on their six-hour tour driving up for their briefing from the Ambassador, ready from the moment they landed to go home and say, yes I saw the revolution and, by God, we've got to do something about those communists or the whole continent will go down the Soviet tube.

I think that if a census were taken, the internationalist gringos would outnumber the Yankees. At least here, in Managua. But then, one never knows who all the gringos are. I'm not suggesting there are spies among them. After all, one could see the spies, with thick necks, blond, close-cropped hair, short-sleeved white shirts and plain grey polyester pants, peering out at us from behind the bars of their cage. No, it's not that. But one doesn't know if everybody is a Northamerican or not. Once when the crowd was larger than usual, we were treated to a sudden burst of Germans who had been lurking about disguised as Northamericans, and who suddenly chained themselves to the gates of the Embassy as a protest against the kidnapping of their countrymen and women by the contras. That was fun! – though not for the ever-serious Sandinista police who were put in the embarrassing position of having to arrest their allies and protect their enemies. One slip, and the provocation longed for by Washington would be at hand. (Mob Attacks US Embassy! Sandinistas Fail to Protect US Property! Remember Grenada! Remember the Maine! Here Comes the Invasion!: I imagine the headlines already written and sitting somewhere in the computer.) Still, it was fun, especially when one of the Germans absconded with the gigantic chain cutter being gamely wielded by one of the serious policemen, and precipitated a wild Keystone Kops chase into the shantytown across the road from the Embassy.

THE VISA

Once, toward the beginning of my stay, I managed to enter the sanctum of the Embassy. Well, not really. But I did more than stand on the street and look at the marines through the bars. Of course, I didn't go through the main gate. There is a side door to the Embassy, where the outpost of Northamerican civilization is invaginated, to permit the entry of natives who wish to do business with the United States Government. And it was there I intruded upon the space of my own country in Nicaragua.

I did so on behalf of Miriam, who needed a visa. Miriam Loisaga is a thirty-year-old Managuan woman, who manages to look both delicate and feisty at the same time, and is one of the geniuses of the revolution. Were it not for the Sandinistas, claims Miriam, she would today be selling cloth in the Mercado Oriental and living through her three children. Instead, she took part in the uprising in the eastern barrios, tending to wounded fighters and smuggling medicines to them under the eyes of the Guardia Nacional. After the triumph, Miriam found her way into the fledgling media enterprise of the revolution, first in INCINE, the Nicaraguan Film Institute, whose films she took into the countryside to show to the peasants; and later as a worker for the Ministry of Agriculture in its cultural and research arm, Midinra. Here her gifts were recognized and she was initiated into the art of video production. From hawking goods in the market, Miriam began to express the unspoken voice of the Nicaraguan people. Her lyrical videotapes documented the transformation of the Nicaraguan peasantry. It was a manifestation of the collective revolutionary subject, Miriam finding her own voice as she found the peasants.

Her work attracted the attention of the independent video community in the United States, who invited her on a speaking tour of several universities in New York and Southern California. The trip was put together in the usual frantic and financially marginal way – compounded in this instance by the exquisite difficulties in communicating with Nicaragua. The US Embassy in Managua had been approached several months in advance to clear Miriam's path to the United States, but to nobody's surprise had done nothing. The upshot was a thoroughly typical cliff-hanger: Miriam's flight was on Thursday, the speaking tour to begin two days later. And on Monday, three days before departure, she had to begin obtaining the necessary clearance from the authorities. This meant, as a practical matter, that Miriam had seventy-two hours to obtain a visa from the United States Embassy. In any other country this would have posed little obstacle. But Miriam was a represent-ative of Ronald Reagan's Devil; except for the curious fact of having an embassy in Managua, the United States was at war with Nicaragua, and one does not ordinarily dispense visas to quasi-official representatives of an enemy government.

'This is crazy,' I had said to my associates in the independent video community before my departure. 'She doesn't speak a word of English, she's never travelled outside the country. She doesn't know her way around the system. All the Embassy has to do is to stall, and Miriam's trip is down the drain.'

'Of course,' was the reply. 'What do you think they've been doing all along? But you'll be down there then; maybe you can help her.'

'Sure, I'll just use my clout at the US Embassy. They'll be most impressed.'

'Do what you can. You know we have to fight these bastards every inch of the way, or nothing will ever happen.'

And that is how I came to try to help Miriam Loisaga get to the United States. We met in front of the side entrance on Monday afternoon, Miriam sedate and formal in a flowered dress, and took our place in the line of supplicants. The marine at the door glanced quizzically at my passport and waved me through without further questioning. I had a sudden burst of disorientation. This zone of enmity was *my* Embassy, literally so. I was a citizen of the United States, and the citizenry, or people, are sovereign. Remember how the Constitution goes: 'We the people . . .', in order to do this and that, are setting up a government to be called the United States of America. It's *our* government: my government. I owned it as much as Ronald Reagan, and the Embassy was my property. In fact, Reagan was fundamentally my employee. So there.

165

The waiting room could have been the Motor Vehicle Bureau in the Bronx, or the Post Office. Same benches and counters. And the same pictures. Such nice-looking men, Reagan and Bush! What fine specimens of Aryan virility they are, with their thin lips and little crinkles about the eyes. It made for such a warm, friendly smile. Afterwards, one could browse through the photos of athletes affixed to a cabinet in the rear of the room, and marvel at the giants from the North, many of them black, each at least one-and-a-half times the volume of the average Comandante.

There were about twenty sombre Nicaraguans ahead of us awaiting their dispensation, but the line moved swiftly, and it was less than an hour before Miriam's name was called. Two male officers were handling the traffic, supported by a number of female clerks. One of the officers was thin, bespectacled and sandy-complexioned and could have been taken for a Sunday school teacher. The other was a different sort altogether. In fact, he could have passed for Nicaraguan were it not for the suggestion of a swagger and a slight smile of amusement which played about the corner of his mouth. In any event he was a Latino. Initially, with a kind of reverse racism, I hoped Miriam would be chosen by one of her own kind rather than the Sunday school teacher who, despite his mild and inoffensive bearing, did look rather too much like George Bush. A brief reflection turned this option on its head, however. Nobody was going to be harder on Miriam than a Latino foreign service officer eager to prove his bona fides to the Yankee master. Anyhow, it was up to chance, and there was nothing to do but see in which direction the receptionist was going to point.

She pointed in the direction of the Latino. Worse luck, thought I, deciding in a wave of apprehension to hold back and let Miriam start off on her own. I had never been clear whether my intervention was going to make matters worse or not. After all, the government would want to keep Miriam out of the United States precisely to the extent that her presence would strengthen the hand of the anti-intervention and solidarity movements. What was this guy going to think when he saw one of the pesky contingent of pro-Sandinistas shepherding her through immigration? Of course, it wasn't as if the purpose of her trip could be kept a secret. Miriam had a letter of introduction from the committee in the United

States, composed in vague and uplifting language and emphasizing the purely artistic interest which her work had aroused; and it was on the basis of this that she was asking for the visa. But nobody was going to be fooled by the stratagem, least of all the Yankee Embassy. Simply by her example, Miriam was going to make things worse for Ronald Reagan and by extension, this foreign service officer. Forget about her tapes. Who could watch this sweet and brilliant person, elevated from the life of petty commerce to that of art by the revolution, and retain the satanic image which Reagan would have the people of the United States believe about Nicaragua? The officer had every reason in the world to try to shoot down her application, whether or not I assisted her. My immediate presence was going to have some kind of effect, no doubt, but it could go either way. So much is decided by ultimately accidental mixes of personal chemistries.

Having decided there was no way of predicting whether I could help Miriam or not, I held back, partly on tactical grounds but mostly because I wanted nothing to do with the swaggering and vaguely sardonic man behind the counter. I was not to get off the hook, however, for after a minute of passing papers back and forth, the officer began to knit his brows. His frown grew and his face darkened as the meaning of Miriam's visit dawned upon him. Miriam turned and looked pleadingly in my direction, like a doe who had just encountered a mountain lion; and as she did, the officer followed her gaze and met mine.

The next thing I knew I was walking toward the counter. 'Can I be of help? This woman is a friend of mine, and I thought I might act as her translator if she needed help. She's never travelled much, you know.'

The officer looked suspiciously at me. 'Who are you? What are you doing here? Where's your passport? And what's the meaning of this?' He pointed to the salutation of the letter: 'Estimada compañera Loisaga.'

'What do you mean?' I said, playing dumb.

'Compañera, compañera, that's a revolutionary address, isn't it?'

'I don't know; I'm sure they're just being polite.'

'Sure . . . sure. Anyhow, who are you? What are you doing here, in Nicaragua?'

'I, well I . . . I work here.'

'Work here? For who?'

'I'm a doctor. The Ministry of Health', I blurted, then immediately regretted the words. I could have just as easily – and truthfully – said I was a writer, but some compulsion forced me to put my head in the block. And a compulsion it must have been, for I didn't really officially work for the Ministry of Health, but was an unpaid volunteer.

The officer's sardonic smile had by now returned. 'You're a doctor, an American doctor, and you work for a foreign government. Have you registered with our Embassy? No? Well sir, it is my duty to inform you that you are doing a dangerous thing. Do you know you may be committing a DEPATRIATING ACT?'

'A what!?'

'A depatriating act, something which could cost you your United States citizenship. Sir, I strongly advise you to register your activities with our Embassy. In fact, I would suggest you have a talk with our Ambassador. He would be happy to counsel you.'

I am not very good at repartee. Taken verbally by surprise, the snappy comeback usually doesn't come to me until the conversation is long over. And there was no question I had been taken by surprise. In fact, I would have to say a little wave of panic swept over me at the officer's remarks – a sudden realization I had been swept into a war against my own government, and that what had been envisioned as a bureaucratic game along the lines of getting parking violations cancelled was full of grave danger. What had I got myself into?

There was a calmer train of thought, too, which grew stronger with time, especially after I checked with my Constitutional law friends back home. This was that citizenship is, if not inviolable, certainly a right that far exceeded the threat he posed to it. In fact, what I should have said – and thought of saying ten minutes later when I finally calmed down – was what my reflections upon entering the Embassy had been pointing toward, namely, that as a citizen I was his boss, and he should watch his tongue when talking to someone for whom he worked. But I said nothing beyond a few stammers.

Having put me in my place, the officer turned to Miriam's

application. Affecting an unctuous manner, he explained to us that this was a delicate matter completely beyond his jurisdiction, that such applications have to be cleared through the State Department office of cultural affairs, which meant that the whole affair would have to be referred to Washington for a decision. And this would, of course, take a considerable amount of time. Of course he understood that Miriam did not have a considerable amount of time, but only forty-eight hours, and he realized that this posed something of a problem and indeed threatened the entire speaking tour. Yes, this was quite a problem, but what could one do? Channels were channels, and the United States government had a carefully worked system which had to be obeyed. Needless to add, we would be welcome to check back tomorrow, even if he could promise nothing.

It seemed to me as we walked out that Miriam had seen the valley of the shadow of death.

I did check back the next day, and learned two things: first, that the office was closed on Tuesdays; and second, the officer, whom I shall call Mr Louis, was nowhere to be found.

I suppose I should have thrown in the towel at that point, depriving Mr Louis of further opportunities for gratifying his sadism and occupying myself in more sensible ways. But of course I was not about to do any such thing. There was a principle involved, worth fighting for every inch; there was the fact that because of my poor Spanish I was already feeling somewhat superfluous at the hospital (an ironic commentary on my statement that I worked for the Ministry of Health, for I was beginning to realize that there was little work for me there); and last but assuredly not least, there was the desire for revenge.

And so I appeared after lunch on Wednesday, having instructed Miriam to meet me in mid-afternoon. Once more the marine glanced quizzically at my passport and admitted me, as he must; and once more I entered the fateful chamber. This time the room was bare of Nicaraguans but contained the clerical staff toiling away at their documents. Suspecting that an Embassy cannot tolerate a silent presence, I decided to sit and let them come to me. I had brought Márquez's *El amor en los tiempos del cólera* for the occasion; and with it in one hand and my trusty dictionary in the other, I settled in prominently on the front bench for a long afternoon's siege. At least I would improve my Spanish.

I was aroused from the book after what must have been fifteen minutes by a clerk inquiring as to the nature of my business. I planted myself before the reception desk and explained that I had an appointment with Mr Louis. The clerk shuffled her feet, looked about nervously, and retreated into the rear, returning in a minute or two with the smirking Louis in tow. He hastened to inform me that his labours had not yet borne fruit, but that he was waiting for a call from the State Department in Washington. If I would care to hang around for a while, he would be pleased to make another call for me; otherwise he could do nothing.

Splendid. I would wait. And I returned to my bench and resumed my Márquez, certain that Louis was only toying with me and only wanted to waste some more of my time. I resolved to give it an hour, no more or less, such being only a few minutes more than the span of silence years of psychoanalytic work had conditioned me to endure.

The hour passed with no sign of activity from the other side of the counter. Disgusted, I resolved to give it another five minutes. Three of these had passed when the clerk suddenly materialized and asked me to come inside. I stumbled after her as in a dream until we came to a little cubbyhole of an office. I sat down and faced, across a desk, Mr Louis looking considerably more agitated than before.

'Look,' he began without introduction, 'I think it only fair to let you know why we're doing this. It's not that the State Department wants to give you people a hard time. But it's the Sandinistas . . . we have to reciprocate for what they do to us.'

'What they do to you . . .?'

'Yes, if you only knew. You know, I just wish some of you guys would listen to us for a while, instead of all that propaganda they feed you. You really should come to the Ambassador's briefings. Then you would learn something about this so-called revolution. Anyhow, they make our life hell here. Why just this week they cut back on the amount of mail we're allowed. We're like prisoners here. So we have to retaliate, make it hard to get visas for the Party members.'

'Party members? Who ever said Miriam Loisaga was a Party member?'

'Come on, who're you kidding? I saw what that letter said: "Compañera Loisaga" . . . that's a sure sign that someone is in the Frente.'

'But Miriam isn't in the party. I can vouch for it. She's not even very political. And barely educated; goes to college at night, raises three children. Where do you think she finds time for the FSLN? Miriam just makes video tapes. She's an artist, and her work isn't very ideological at all. And to call someone here a *compañera* is just a sign of respect. You know, the people here admire their revolutionaries.'

In fact, I couldn't literally vouch at that moment for Miriam's non-membership in the *Frente*, though it seemed unquestionable (and was in fact true). In any case I was playing for time. The whole thing began to take on a sporting quality in which I sensed the upper hand. Behind the braggadocio was obviously a rather foolish and insecure young man. The way to go was to string him along, play to his vanity, keep my own hand obscure. The longer this went on, the better would it go for me.

Louis snorted. 'That's a lot of bullshit, the whole revolutionary thing. You should know what these guys are really like. How many assassinations each of the comandantes is responsible for, how they have people they don't like gunned down in the street. You know what one of our biggest jobs here is? Protecting Nicaraguans with dual citizenship. Whenever one of these kids comes down here to visit, the state security police tries to kidnap them. Then they put them in the army.'

'I didn't know that.'

'That's right; there's a whole lot you don't know.' The smirk was in full bloom. 'This whole revolution. What a failure! A lost chance to do some good for these poor people. But they broke all the promises . . . turned on the real democrats, and went the Soviet way. Now they're worse than Somoza ever was. Everything is controlled by the military here, or the police. They have all the supplies and they keep it for themselves, and crush all dissent. Real totalitarians, that's right.'

'Here's where I would have to take exception to what you're saying. These are pretty amazing people here; and if you got to know them instead of being the mouthpiece for the US line, you might see things a little differently. Maybe you should think about what the US has done to this country, and what it takes to get you off their backs. Anyway, you should see the videotapes Miriam makes; and how the peasants really live a new life. We could show them to you.'

'We can't have communist propaganda coming into the United States. These guys like Borge come up and denounce Yankee imperialism and all that shit. I mean, we don't need that.'

'But Miriam doesn't have any kind of ideological line. Anyhow what can the United States fear from this woman? What are you guys afraid of, anyway?'

And so we went for many minutes, jawing back and forth about the virtues of the Sandinist revolution and the threat that it, or rather, Miriam Loisaga, posed to the most powerful nation on earth. In itself, it was a tedious discussion, and was certainly not going to change anybody's attitude. In fact, I couldn't understand why Louis was allowing it to go on at all in view of our mutual intransigence and the fact I had everything to gain by prolonging the discussion. There was an underlying tension I couldn't get at.

Suddenly, Louis's manner became more cordial and he changed the subject. 'And so what do you do back in the States?' I said I was a professor at a medical school, and he excitedly interjected that his father was also a professor at a medical school, to wit, Columbia.

'Isn't that interesting?' I added, 'I went to Columbia medical school.'

'Hey, no kidding!' blurted Louis. He became even more excited when he learned I lived in Manhattan. 'That's where I grew up, on the Upper West Side. What do you know? A professor at a medical school!'

I felt compelled to tell him that I was in the process of switching jobs, and that in the autumn I would be a Professor of Political Science.

'Another coincidence! I majored in Political Science ... at Fordham, in the Bronx. I used to argue with my professors all the time. They were so liberal. That's when I became so right-wing. It was Allende; I was glad he got what he did. He deserved it. Do you know what that bastard was planning? Massacres, that's what. It's a good thing the coup came when it did. Saved a lot of lives.' A pause. 'Say, tell me, I hope you won't mind my asking, suppose you were my professor right now, would you flunk me for the argument I was just giving?'

I was aware of some disingenuousness as I replied, 'No, I don't think so, even though I strongly disagree with you . . .'

But he would not let me finish, and as if determined to force his condemnation, continued: 'But suppose I was a Nazi? Would you fail me then?'

I saw I had to give in. 'Well, of course, in that case, yes. Because if you were a Nazi, you wouldn't be using the rules of evidence or logic. And that's unacceptable in the classroom.'

Another pause. 'I see your point.'

Our discourse had turned upside-down. The once supercilious official of the United States Department of State had become an embarrassed youth. His face flushed, Louis's argument began cascading downhill: 'Well, I don't know if I should be doing this . . . giving you guys a chance . . . you know I could lose my job if I gave out this visa. I mean, really, if this woman goes up North and starts spouting off the communist line, I could really be in trouble . . .'

There was no mention of the long-awaited call from Washington. I felt it would be somewhat indelicate of me to remind Louis of this fact and confined myself to reassuring him of Miriam's non-ideological qualities.

'Well, all right, I'm going to do it, that's all. Just this once.' And he pulled out a pad of visa forms from his desk, wrote on the top one, stamped it a few times and affixed the visa to Miriam's passport, which had been in front of him all the while.

I took the passport and thanked him for his services, adding as I left the room: 'This job obviously means a lot to you, but if you want to know my opinion, I think it would be a blessing for you if you were fired. Frankly, you would be better off in another career. You're working for some awful people.'

Miriam was waiting outside in the hot Managua sun. We celebrated with an ice cream, at a special place she showed me on the Pista de la Resistencia. Her trip was a great success . . . not without a few hitches, of course.

THE BREAKDOWN

On various occasions the cars I drove in Nicaragua failed to start, stalled in the middle of the road, were without radiator caps, developed malfunctioning doors which could not be closed or flew open in traffic, had the retread fly off the tyre, were without a windshield wiper motor, lost a wiper blade in a rainstorm after the motor was installed, leaked fluid from the differential, needed main wheel bearings for the front end, and snapped a main engine bearing in the middle of the Pista, the latter mishap causing the engine to separate from the transmission, with a negative effect on the car's locomotive power. In fact, one could hardly call these vehicles – I lived with three of them, all the property of Ezra H – *automobiles*, so frequently did they have to be towed, pushed or just left in the middle of the road.

But the worst was what happened on the road to Selva Negra, north of Matagalpa.

We had set out in the Monte Carlo, Ezra, Kenia, baby Solmaría and myself, for a weekend jaunt at the famous resort high in the coffee country. The Monte Carlo was the biggest of the cars, and the one I hated the most. It was a brutal, clunky vehicle, and needless to say, of pre-1979 vintage. We called it the Somozamobile. I recently saw a Monte Carlo advertised in a 1976 *National Geographic*, and it stunned me to see how elegant Chevrolet made that thing out to be. Now it stood, like Shelley's Ozymandias or Gloria Swanson in *Sunset Boulevard*, a ruined monument to time and illusion. But it was big, perhaps bigger than the other two cars combined – a 1967 Renault which looked like a refugee from *M. Hulot's Holiday*, and a 1977 Honda Civic. And for this reason it remained the car of choice for trips outside Managua.

We set off on a hot dusty Friday afternoon, late, and eager to get to the mountains beyond Matagalpa before dark. The road north from Managua is reasonably good and, though the main highway of the country, scarcely travelled; and there was power to spare beneath the Monte Carlo's immense hood. With hopes high, we sped north.

The land is level for a spell, then rises in a series of plateaux. The first of these is announced by a very long hill, not very steep in itself but of such great length as to pose a severe strain to all but the healthiest cars. The Monte Carlo was not such a car. As we climbed and climbed, I began to get an odd sensation, as in a story by Poe when the muffled sound is heard from deep within the haunted house. Something was wrong.

'Do you hear a noise?' Ezra asked. 'From below.'

'Yes, I think so, but I can't quite place it.'

And then it began in earnest: Ping . . . ping . . . ping: softly but insistently, and accompanied by great clouds of blue and white smoke. Very picturesque. 'Ezra, I think we're in trouble.'

We pulled to a stop and inspected the damage. A lot of the smoke was coming from the radiator, which turned out to be near-empty; but there was another source, the blue one, from under the engine, which was clearly more ominous. A group of children materialized, and through them we were able to obtain enough water to proceed. But the question was, in which direction? Back to Managua, which was home, mostly downhill, and where some services would be available? Or on to Matagalpa, which was about the same distance, might possibly have services, being the third or fourth most populous city in Nicaragua, and where our weekend awaited us? True, it was mostly uphill, but that made it cooler, not an inconsiderable factor in view of the relentless Managua heat.

So we went on to Matagalpa. It was the courageous thing to do.

The pinging let up for a while, then began again. It seemed to be cyclical; and I began to console myself with the idea that this might be just the way the car had decided to work. Who knows how long it could go on pinging like that? Months, maybe . . . these old American cars were creaky and clumsy, but they lasted forever.

The mechanic in Matagalpa, where we pulled up at dusk, said more or less the same thing. He had crawled under the Monte Carlo, listened to the pinging, tapped a few times on the underworks, and pronounced the machine fit. Probably should last until we got back to Managua; but if there was any problem, come on by tomorrow.

And so we set off on the fifteen kilometres to Selva Negra under a rapidly darkening sky. Now if the hills up to Matagalpa are long and gentle, the hills beyond Matagalpa are fierce, steep and jagged. It is the most picturesque part of Nicaragua, which is why we wanted to go there in the first place. Unfortunately, picturesqueness correlates positively with difficulty of driving; and it became apparent after one kilometre of those hills that we were in for a disaster.

The Monte Carlo may have lasted seven kilometres, but I don't know how. It must have been sheer grit, because there seemed to be no mechanical grounds for proceeding. As Ezra yelled to put the car in third gear, and I yelled to keep it in first, and Kenia and the baby maintained a discreet silence, we floundered about like a beached whale, until with a final gasp and shudder, the Monte Carlo gave up the ghost. We were stranded in the Nicaraguan countryside, in territory infested with the contra. Not that we were worried. We were in Nicaragua, and in Nicaragua one is never alone. Indeed, after five minutes a quite serviceable Toyota van picked us up and took us to the resort – which happened to be considerably out of the driver's way. We were then driven back to the Monte Carlo by one of the hotel's employees, to remove our gear. The problem along this stretch of road, we were told, is not contras, but thieves; like vultures, they would pick any unguarded car clean, tyres and all. A *campesino* then materialized, as if fetched by a security agency. Naturally, he would be delighted to sit in our car and guard it for the night. The fee: 1,000 córdobas (worth a dollar at the official rate of exchange, half that much on the black market). All he needed was a minute, to run home and fetch his machete. We left him sitting locked inside the car, machete prominently displayed rising from between his legs.

Selva Negra means Black Forest, and is so named because the region was developed by Germans. A group of nine of these pioneers is immortalized in a huge and grotesque mural over the fireplace in the main lodge, the white lords looking stiff and uncomfortable amidst the railroad they had built to haul their coffee out of the mountains. The resort itself was owned by one of their descendants, a woman said to be an ardent supporter of the contra, who occasionally came by for provisions and moral support. Bursts of gunfire could be heard in the surrounding hills throughout the weekend, leading me to wonder whether some more of the *dueña*'s pals would be paying us a call. However I was reassured that the noise level was routine.

176

When the contras are away, the place is much favoured by Western businessmen, schoolteachers and diplomatic staffs, including those of the United States Embassy, a considerable contingent of whom had already gathered, families in tow, for their weekend away from the blazing capital. The gossip was about the impending confiscation of Selva Negra by the Sandinistas, a process which those assembled saw, along with the continuous attrition of their own prime dwellings in the hills surrounding Managua, strictly as another instance of communist perfidy. Chatting with them was not what I had had in mind for a pleasant weekend, nor was the invitation to join their weekly bridge game back in Managua, but I was definitely, if fortuitously, stuck with these folks for the time being.

Because there was no way I could see of getting back to Managua in the Monte Carlo. More, I could not conceive what could be done with the Monte Carlo at all. It was plain the automatic transmission had blown, and there is no more difficult part of a car to repair, especially in Nicaragua. Leave it, I supposed with the habit of mind of a throwaway culture, until its bleached bones should dry in the sun. In fact, there seemed no point in even having the car guarded. It had to be abandoned to the forces of entropy; and if these came quickly and historically, in the guise of thieves, rather than slowly and organically, as the elements of nature, what was the difference? The car was a goner, that was all.

Still, one had to go through the motions. And so Ezra and I hitched a ride to Matagalpa the next morning with one of the Yankees, there to try our luck with the northern Nicaraguan facilities for auto repair. And the first thing we discovered was that there was neither road service nor towing service in Matagalpa. Nor in all of Nicaragua outside Managua, one hundred kilometres away, for that matter. Of course, I couldn't see what a towing service could do anyway with the Monte Carlo, perched precipitously close to the edge of a steep mountain road. I think I was secretly glad at this, so much did I hate that car.

'Well, that takes care of that,' I said to Ezra. 'We can kiss the Somozamobile good-bye.'

Just then a man who had been leaning nearby against a battered-looking Toyota truck spoke up. 'Why don't we try the EPS? They have a base near here, and some big trucks on it, IFAs. They should be able to tow your car.'

I recalled the base, about six kilometres to the south. We had seen it while driving up, a collection of tents atop a sandy knoll. I vaguely remembered the huge East German vehicles, the scourge of Nicaragua's roads, parked there. Instinctively, from countless frightening impressions of IFAs hurtling through the streets of Managua, I wanted nothing to do with any of the adolescents who had been given charge of these monsters.

'The army? Why ask them?'

'Come on, it's the only hope you have. We have nothing to lose.'

And so we bundled into the yellow Toyota truck, the Samaritan chatting amiably as he drove. There was a little guardhouse at the entrance to the army compound where we waited while a pair of young soldiers checked our papers. Their superior, a lieutenant who looked barely old enough to shave, arrived, and the Samaritan, who seemed to know him, introduced me as an *internacionalista* doctor who was serving the revolution and whose *carro* was in distress. Could they help? The lieutenant stared at the floor for a few seconds, nodded, and invited us to wait inside his office until the tow-truck should arrive. We waited half-an-hour, talking with a local citizen about imperialism and revolution under a diagram of a Soviet tank and a stern-looking poster of the Ortega brothers. Then we were led outside to the waiting IFA tow-truck.

It was titanic, quite the largest ground-based machine I ever saw in Nicaragua, and after wheezing and clanking up the mountain road, it picked up the Monte Carlo as if it were a toy car – not without a great deal of backing and filling and teetering over the edge of the cliff, however – and gently pulled it down the mountainside into Matagalpa. We bought lunch for the two teenage soldier-drivers, bid them farewell, and took a cab back to Selva Negra. When I told one of the women from the United States Embassy of our good fortune, she shrugged and said, 'So what? It just proves that the army has everything in Nicaragua . . .'

As we sat in the guardhouse waiting for the lieutenant, I had felt the eyes of one of the soldiers upon me. Actually, he was looking at my chest, and smiling shyly. I looked back and smiled uncertainly in return. Then his companion remarked with a laugh: 'He likes your jacket. He'd like you to give it to him.'

This made the boy blush and avert his gaze. I mumbled and looked down, not knowing how to reply, but vaguely indicating the inappropriateness of the request. Happily, the arrival of the lieutenant rescued me from the situation. It could not, however, stay the current of my thought, which raced on all the while we waited for the IFA tow-truck.

Of course, it was out of the question. This youngster was nothing to me; nobody but he and his fellow guard even knew the request had been made; and he would be quite happy to forget the whole embarrassing incident. Of this I was certain. In fact, there was no *quid pro quo* in the transaction, since the soldier's desire for my jacket had preceded any negotiations with the lieutenant, or even any mention of our straits. It was simply his desire, no more.

The facts of the matter were quite simple. I was wearing an old military castoff shirt jacket, of British manufacture, made from high quality heavy cotton, and of the same olive colour as Nicaraguan military gear. The boy's garment, by comparison, was shoddy. The cut of the cloth, the way it lay on his body – everything indicated inferior goods. I don't know who makes the clothes for the Ejército Popular Sandinista, but they don't hold a candle to the British. Why, my jacket had been made well before the soldier had been born – back in the fifties, I think. I had been wearing it myself for a good half of the soldier's life, and it looked a lot sharper than his own shirt. No wonder he wanted it. And no wonder I wanted to hold onto it.

As we sat in the lieutenant's office, chatting about whether the United States people really supported Reagan's policies toward Nicaragua, I thought of this, and more besides. It was clear that there was a virtue to the jacket which greatly exceeded any manifest value. I loved it, the way we love things of quality and service, for its roughness and its indestructibility. It had been everywhere with me, on every hike, every trip abroad. I had worn it alone, had worn sweaters under it and overclothes over it. I am relatively indifferent to what I wear, but there are exceptions, and this jacket was a major one. It was more than a garment; it was part of myself. It was more than a possession, more than property: it was me. It's mine, I thought, why should I give it to this stranger? Nothing would be gained by so doing; they're going to rescue the Monte Carlo with the IFA whether or not I give the jacket to this unknown Nicaraguan boy. Its mine . . . mine . . . mine . . . mine . . .

The lieutenant came to announce the arrival of the IFA. We walked, blinking, into the hot midday sun, past the guardhouse. I turned, peeled off the jacket, and pushed it into the hands of the startled soldier. Nothing was said, though I felt them looking at me as I went on, toward the tow-truck and up into its gigantic frame.

I felt exalted after this event. But later, after I had written it down, I recalled a scene from Rossellini's film about St Francis where the saint admonishes a follower who has a compulsion to give his clothing away to the poor. It is not enough, Francis was saying, in effect, to prove one's virtue through an act of philanthropy. There is a spiritual pride in the giver which will remain so long as there are barriers between people. And this is another reason why there is no end to revolutions.

EPILOGUE

The man sitting next to me on the TACA flight from San Salvador was so corpulent I had to turn away from him to fit into my seat. But one cannot remain that isolated for a two-and-a-half-hour flight, and after some bumping and squirming, we were led to converse. He was an amiable fellow, on his way back to Wisconsin from El Salvador, where he had been looking into the possibility of restarting a defunct gold mine. The Duarte government had had some success in pacifying the region in which the mine was located. This gave him some confidence that profits would start rolling his way again from El Salvador. But he didn't know; on the whole, the trip had not been successful. Terrible bureaucracy, inefficiency, corruption. One can't do anything in these banana republics.

I decided to make him a test case of my *compromiso*, or pact, with the Nicaraguan people: to carry the word of their tribulation and heroism to my fellow citizens. What better place to start?

And so I expatiated at length on the situation in Nicaragua, emphasizing the distance between the reality of the country and the images we have been fed about it, stressing the need for each American to think fearlessly and free of stereotypes or labels. He listened attentively and, it seemed, sympathetically. Then he said: 'But they're communists, aren't they?'

'I don't know what you mean by that.' (A carefully thought out gambit, designed to induce critical reflection.)

'I mean they are communists down there. And that means they should get out and go back to Russia where they belong, and leave the country to people who can develop the economy properly.'

'But Nicaragua is their country', I replied weakly.

'I don't care,' he shot back. 'If they are communists, they belong in Russia.'

In the Miami airport, the newsmagazines were celebrating Miss Liberty and the Fourth of July.

Two weeks later: Washington in the morning. We had driven down from New York for a rally and civil disobedience at the Capitol protesting against contra aid: a long hot drive to find less than five hundred protesters. But it is the last chance to prevent the Senate from ratifying the 100 million dollars. We were early, and decided to use the time to show Molly what Congress looked like. I remembered visiting the gallery as a boy, in 1948, with my father . . . and the awe we felt; the feeling of unity with the great project of representative democracy. This was our government. The Congressional offices are still wonderfully accessible, the passes for the asking. (Though this produced some disillusionment. Had it been that easy for my father? I had thought we must have been very special to get into the Senate gallery.)

But to get into the Chamber is like undertaking the Stations of the Cross. No, worse: one feels like cattle in the stockyard, herded from pen to pen. Line after line, winding ever higher into the innermost sanctum. On one landing I counted 140 people, three of them black: perhaps a statistical fluke. At the penultimate line a tour guide appears, gives us a wisecracking speech, each joke sculpted to perfection. No this is not a church, not a stockyard: this is DISNEYWORLD. Finally we get into the Senate Chamber, to find it nearly bereft of Senators. The gallery, however, is full of craning citizens in plaid shorts and jumpers, children holding their dolls or waving flags and pennants. We get to see Barry Goldwater, reciting to empty seats some part of the military appropriations bill to which contra aid is a codicil. We must keep America strong, Goldwater intones, to protect her against her enemies.

Then we have to leave. Time for the demonstration. Our seats are immediately filled.

We hear more Senators on the steps of the Capitol than we saw inside the Chamber. Cranston, Simon, Harkin come forward to speak against contra aid, as does Governor Anaya of New Mexico, various officials of the District of Columbia and Church leaders. Charles Liteky, who had been a chaplain in Vietnam, comes forward to renounce his Congressional Medal of Honor and to announce his forthcoming fast on behalf of suffering Nicaragua. The civil disobedience inside the Rotunda goes well: witness has been borne.

Later, as we leave, we pass a group of uniformed schoolgirls, evidently from the South. We overhear them chatting and giggling: 'Did y'all see those demonstrators? They are WEIRD! Stay away from them, heah!'

I replace my jacket. The secondhand shops are gone; or perhaps I have lost patience. Then I find an acceptable substitute, though new and expensive. I know the store in advance: Banana Republic. Where else?

At least I get to cut out the label.

185

This first edition of
In Nicaragua
was finished in September 1988.

It was set in 10/13 Sabon Roman,
on a Linotron 202,
printed on a Crabtree NP56 Offset-litho press
on 80g/m^2 vol. 18 Supreme book wove.

The book was commissioned and
edited by Robert M. Young,
copy-edited by Elizabeth Thomas,
designed by Wendy Millichap,
and produced by Martin Klopstock and
Selina O'Grady for
Free Association Books.